REGION Volume 4, Number 2, 2017

Well-being in cities and regions: Measurement, analysis and policy practices

Special Issue edited by **Paolo Veneri** and **Arjen J.E. Edzes**

Table of Contents

This special issue on "Well-being in cities and regions: measurement, analysis and policy practices" is edited by Paolo Veneri (OECD, Paris, France) and Arjen J.E. Edzes (University of Groningen, Groningen, The Netherlands). With the exception of the editorial, all contributions to this special issue have already been published in earlier issues of REGION, for the sake of immediate exposure of the content.

- *Subjective Wellbeing Impacts of National and Subnational Fiscal Policies* by Arthur Grimes, Judd Ormsby, Anna Robinson and Siu Yuat Wong was originally published in vol. 3, no. 1, 43–69.

- *Happiness in Romanian cities on the road from post-communism transition to EU accession* by Camilla Lenzi and Giovanni Perucca was originally published in vol. 3, no. 2, 1–22.

- *Pride and the city* by Philip S. Morrison was originally published in vol. 3, no. 2, 103–124.

- *Cities and Inequality* by Alessandra Michelangeli and Eugenio Peluso was originally published in vol. 3, no. 2, 47–60.

REGION, The journal of ERSA / Powered by WU
ISSN: 2409-5370, ISBN: 978-3-9504846-0-1

ERSA: http://www.ersa.org
WU: http://www.wu.ac.at

Editorials

The Journal of ERSA
Powered by WU

Volume 4, Number 2, 2017, E1-E5
DOI: 10.18335/region.v4i2.188

journal homepage: region.ersa.org

Editorial:
Well-being in cities and regions: Measurement, analysis and policy practices*

Paolo Veneri[1], Arjen J.E. Edzes[2]

[1] Organisation for Economic Co-operation and Development (OECD), Paris, France (email: paolo.veneri@oecd.org)
[2] University of Groningen, Groningen, The Netherlands (email: a.j.e.edzes@rug.nl)

Received: 19 January 2017/Accepted: 19 January 2017

Abstract. This note introduces the special issue on Well-being in cities and regions: measurement, analysis and policy practices. After highlighting the importance of well-being research, this contribution provides a rationale for focusing on the local level rather than looking at country averages for both analytical and policy purposes. While introducing the papers in this Special Issue, we highlight the need to focus on the regional and local factors that improve people's well-being and the need to understand the link between objective and subjective measures of well-being so that better use is made of them in policy making.

1 Introduction: why measure well-being?

The use of Gross Domestic Product (GDP) and, more generally, of conventional economic indicators to orientate policy making and to measure progress in society has been progressively decreasing in recent years. Behind this trend are several factors, which have been extensively discussed in the scientific debate (Brezzi et al. 2016). First, GDP gives only a partial picture of societal progress. While it allows the "quantitative" side of economic growth to be assessed, it does not give much information on its "qualitative" side. Second, GDP does not say much about how societies are evolving in a sustainable way from both an environmental and a social point of view – for instance, about how inequality interacts with aggregate well-being. Moreover, economic growth is increasingly disconnected from life satisfaction, especially in the most developed countries (Di Tella, MacCulloch 2010). This disconnection started with the so-called Easterlin paradox, according to which a positive cross-country relationship between life satisfaction and aggregate income (when measured at one point in time) coexisted with a non-significant relationship between happiness and aggregate income in time-series analysis (Easterlin 1995). Recent evidence shows a hump-shaped relationship between aggregate income and life satisfaction –at both national and regional level – with a positive shape only for the countries or regions with relatively low income levels (Proto, Rustichini 2013).

The scientific and policy importance of measuring well-being has been further highlighted by some major international initiatives, such as the work of the Commission

---

*The views expressed herein are those of the authors and do not reflect those of the OECD or its member countries.

on the Measurement of Economic Performance and Social Progress, which resulted in a flagship report published in 2009 (Stiglitz et al. 2009), or, in the same year, the EU Communication on 'GDP and Beyond'. Two years later, the OECD launched its Better Life Initiative, which provides a concrete framework and data for comparing well-being outcomes across OECD countries (Durand 2015, OECD 2015). These initiatives have been followed by other national ones, which have taken different forms, from public consultations to parliamentary commissions or, in many cases, statistical work undertaken by National Statistical Offices. Overall, these works – primarily those of the so-called Stiglitz-Sen-Fitoussi Commission – have identified some major points for a statistical agenda to improve the measurement of well-being. Among these points are the need to focus on people (i.e. individuals and households), rather than on the wide economic system; to acknowledge the multidimensional nature of well-being, which requires coverage of many aspects that are important for people's lives; to account for the distribution of well-being outcomes across all social groups, rather than focusing on simple averages; and to reconcile the objective measures of well-being with those based on individual perceptions, which reflect how people actually experience and assess their life circumstances.

2 Why measure well-being at the scale of cities and regions?

The importance of well-being measures is ultimately explained by their use in the policy-making process. In this regard, one crucial aspect of any well-being indicator is the geographic scale to which that indicator refers. The territorial element underlying well-being measures has a crucial role to play in moving public policy from a simple measurement perspective to an action-oriented one. More specifically, there are several reasons why it is important to measure well-being at the local level.

First of all, it should be considered that people's well-being is shaped by a combination of individual traits and place-based characteristics (OECD 2014). Some of the dimensions of well-being are strongly dependent on the context in which the individual lives, such as environmental quality, safety conditions, the dynamism of the labour market, and the cohesion and civic engagement of the community. This perspective becomes crucial when considering that well-being outcomes are not evenly distributed across space in most countries. In the OECD, differences in well-being outcomes among the regions of the same country are often remarkable, being similar to or even larger than those found across countries. This is the case, for example, of the unemployment rate in Italian regions or of the years of life expectancy across the different states in the US (OECD 2016). These differences can be very important in regard to the living conditions experienced by individuals in their everyday lives.

The literature highlights that specific spatial factors can have a role in individual's well-being. Ballas (2013) argues that certain contextual factors, such as income level and its distribution within the city, or social justice, are increasingly important for subjective well-being. Rodríguez-Pose, Maslauskaite (2011) find that, besides individual and macroeconomic factors, institutional characteristics are crucial for people's life satisfaction. Such characteristics refer to issues that are often very place-specific, such as trust in the institutions, the quality of local government, or the extent to which public expenditure or taxation is decentralised to subnational levels of government. Other scholars have highlighted the importance of the spatial organisation of cities for well-being. Brown et al. (2015) found that overall residential density and land-use fragmentation are negatively correlated with life satisfaction. Moreover, urban size has been found to be detrimental to life satisfaction (Okulicz-Kozaryn 2015). These results open the way for further research on the place-based dimension of well-being.

Second, and following the previous points made, regional and local governments have often the discretionary authority for policies that directly affect people's lives. They play an important role in providing services that enhance economic dynamism, safety, health, and so on, and they represent the bulk of public investment. In the OECD, subnational government expenditure accounted for 17% of GDP and 40% of total public expenditure in 2014 (OECD 2016). Local levels of government therefore often have an immediate impact on the well-being of citizens and communities. This relates to people's trust in public institutions and institutional quality, which can play an important role in how the most pressing challenges are tackled and reflected in spatial disparities within countries (Ezcurra, Rodríguez-Pose 2014).

Spatial features can also be important for understanding how different policy domains interact in a single city or region. When different well-being dimensions – such as income, jobs and health – are considered together, advantages and disadvantages tend to amplify the spatial concentration of prosperity or exclusion (Veneri, Murtin 2016). Moreover, most policy interactions are spatially specific: policies on land use, transport and housing, for example, are closely connected to the well-being of individuals and communities. These different strands of policy could achieve better results if they were designed in a way that maximises their complementarities and that manages possible trade-offs better. This can happen only when these aspects are tackled in the specific places where they occur.

3 The papers in this Special Issue and the directions for future research

This Special Issue was primarily inspired by the debates and discussions which took place during the 55th Congress of the European Regional Science Association in Lisbon, on August 2015. In that context, three special sessions were organised to discuss the topic of "Well-being in cities and regions: measurement, analysis and policy practices". The congress also hosted a semi-plenary session on how the measurement of well-being at local level can improve the design of policies. After the event, four papers were selected to be included in this special issue. They cover important aspects of the measurement and analysis of well-being at regional and urban level.

The first paper, by Arthur Grimes, Judd Ormsby, Anna Robinson and Siu Yuat Wong (Grimes et al. 2016), addresses one of the main research issues in the place-based well-being literature: that of understanding the role of institutional conditions as drivers of well-being. The paper provides an analysis on the link between the characteristics of the fiscal policy and subjective well-being in 35 countries. The authors find that while distortionary taxes, such as income taxes, are generally detrimental for economic growth with respect to non-distortionary taxes, distortionary taxes are associated with higher levels of subjective well-being compared with their non-distortionary counterparts. The authors also find that the government expenditures which are considered as "unproductive" – those which do not enter the production side of the economy, but only the utility function of individuals – are associated with higher well-being for the middle class relative to others. In regard to fiscal decentralisation, the authors find that devolving expenditure power to subnational levels of government is associated with higher levels of subjective well-being, while decentralising tax collection shows a negative association. On the other hand, the authors find no mediating effect of the size of settlement on the link between fiscal policy and subjective well-being.

The second paper, by Camilla Lenzi and Giovanni Perucca (Lenzi, Perucca 2016), analyses how differences in subjective well-being between urban and rural areas change over time. More specifically, the authors focus on Romania, a country which in the past 15 years has experienced strong divergences in the economic growth rates of different types of territories. The results of the analysis show that the temporal dimension plays an important role in the link between economic growth and subjective well-being. The Easterlin intuition of a trade-off between economic growth and life satisfaction is found to apply only in some circumstances and not in all places. In the largest cities, economic growth during Romania's period of transition was faster, but subjective well-being showed a relatively lower performance with respect to that of other places. However, this trade-off was not observed in the medium-sized cities, where economic growth was combined with higher life satisfaction. The paper finally suggests that the trade-off between economic growth and well-being is not spatially neutral, and that in some circumstances it is possible to combine the two objectives.

The third paper, by Philip Morrison (Morrison 2016), analyses the spatial dimension of urban pride in New Zealand. Urban pride is an emotion that, unlike life satisfaction, involves stake holding. For this reason, urban pride is a powerful concept with greater relevance to local policy making. When an individual is proud about the city in which s/he lives, this implies that the same individual is making a "place-based" investment in emotional, financial or cultural terms. In other words, proud residents are residents who care about their place, with possible implications for the identification of policy priorities, for the quality of institutions and, ultimately, the effectiveness of policy in enhancing the well-being of each community. The author finds that the degree of urban pride in New Zealand varies primarily according to individual characteristics, although variation across cities is also observed. By using a multilevel model approach, the author finds that city characteristics, although less important than individual traits, affect the way in which different types of stake holding temper urban pride. This is the case, for example, of the aggregate support for city councils, which conditions the effect of residence duration on urban pride. City leaders can be particularly interested in fostering "soft returns" such as urban pride, which remains a very promising and still largely unexplored research issue.

The fourth paper, by Alessandra Michelangeli and Eugenio Peluso (Michelangeli, Peluso 2016), provides a method with which to measure well-being inequality across cities by accounting for the spatial distribution of key urban features, such as public infrastructures, local services, as well as economic and environmental conditions. The authors apply their analysis to the case of Italian cities. Their method is based on the hypothesis that, in a country where amenities are evenly distributed across cities rather than concentrated in a few ones, the average level of well-being is higher. This hypothesis – which is justified by the argument that not all individuals in a society are equally exposed to the same quantities and qualities of amenities due to the spatial concentration of the latter – allows the authors to apply an Atkinson inequality measure approach. The authors use a hedonic approach to derive a monetary evaluation of amenities. The multidimensional index proposed has the advantage that it makes it possible to differentiate the effects of the amenities on the overall degree of inequality, and on the other hand, to consider the joint effect of all amenities on the overall inequality.

We hope that the contributions in this special issue, together with the concepts provided in this note, will stimulate and feed further research on the measurement of well-being at local level, and on how these measures can be of importance for policy making in order to improve people's lives in all places. While the papers presented in this special issue provide some new insights on important issues connected with regional and urban well-being, there are several aspects where research is much needed. Two issues are important. The first is clarification of the concept of well-being. Although it seems that there is a broad consensus in the scientific community on definitions, the four papers show again a wide variety in concepts, definitions and measurement. The second issue is the need to gain better understanding of the link between objective and subjective measures of well-being. Should policy makers pursue the former or the latter? Understanding this link would make it possible to combine the individual and subjective points of view with assessment of the conditions of a community. Because citizens are part of a society, the conditions of the society as a whole, whether in a city or in another local environment, should not be left aside.

References

Ballas D (2013) What makes a 'happy city'? *Cities* 32: S39–S50. CrossRef.

Brezzi M, De Mello L, Laurent E (2016) Au-delà du PIB, en-deçà du PIB. Mesurer le bien-être territorial dans l'OCDE. *Revue de l'OFCE* 145: 13–32. CrossRef.

Brown ZS, Oueslati W, Silva J (2015) Exploring the effect of urban structure on individual well-being. OECD environment working papers 95, OECD Publishing. CrossRef.

Di Tella R, MacCulloch R (2010) Happiness adaptation to income beyond 'basic needs'. In: Diener E, Helliwell J, Kahneman D (eds), *International Differences in Well-Being*. Oxford University Press, Oxford. CrossRef.

Durand M (2015) The OECD better life initiative: How's life and the measurement of well-being. *Review of Income and Wealth* 61: 4–17. CrossRef.

Easterlin RA (1995) Will raising the incomes of all increase the happiness of all? *Journal of Economic Behavior and Organization* 27: 35–47. CrossRef.

Ezcurra R, Rodríguez-Pose A (2014) Government quality and spatial inequality: A cross-country analysis. *Environment and Planning A* 46: 1732–1753. CrossRef.

Grimes A, Ormsby J, Robinson A, Wong SY (2016) Subjective wellbeing impacts of national and subnational fiscal policies. *REGION* 3[1]: 43–69. CrossRef.

Lenzi C, Perucca G (2016) Life satisfaction in Romanian cities on the road from post-communism transition to EU accession. *REGION* 3[2]: 1–22. CrossRef.

Michelangeli A, Peluso E (2016) Cities and inequality. *REGION* 3[2]: 47–60. CrossRef.

Morrison PS (2016) Pride in the city. *REGION* 3[2]: 103–124. (reprinted in this issue)

OECD (2014) How's life in your region? Measuring regional and local well-being for policy making. OECD publishing, Paris. CrossRef.

OECD (2015) How's life? 2015: Measuring well-being. OECD publishing, Paris. CrossRef.

OECD (2016) Regions at a glance 2016. OECD publishing, Paris. CrossRef.

Okulicz-Kozaryn A (2015) *Happiness and place: Why life is better outside of the City*. Palgrave Macmillan, New York. CrossRef.

Proto E, Rustichini A (2013) A reassessment of the relationship between GDP and life satisfaction. *PLoS ONE* 8: e79358. CrossRef.

Rodríguez-Pose A, Maslauskaite K (2011) Can policy make us happier? Individual characteristics, socio-economic factors and life satisfaction in Central and Eastern Europe. *Cambridge Journal of Regions, Economy and Society* 5: 77–96. CrossRef.

Stiglitz JE, Sen A, Fitoussi JP (2009) *Mismeasuring Our Lives: Why GDP Doesn't Add Up. The Report by the Commission on the Measurement of Economic Performance and Social Progress*. The New Press, New York

Veneri P, Murtin F (2016) Where is inclusive growth happening? Mapping multi-dimensional living standards in OECD regions, OECD statistics working papers, No. 2016/01, OECD Publishing, Paris. CrossRef.

Articles

REGION

The Journal of ERSA
Powered by WU

erso WU FWF

Volume 3, Number 1, 2016, 43-69
DOI: 10.18335/region.v3i1.121

journal homepage: region.ersa.org

Subjective Wellbeing Impacts of National and Subnational Fiscal Policies*

Arthur Grimes[1], Judd Ormsby[2], Anna Robinson[3], Siu Yuat Wong[4]

[1] Motu Economic and Public Policy Research, and Victoria University of Wellington, Wellington, New Zealand (email: arthur.grimes@motu.org.nz)
[2] Motu Economic and Public Policy Research, Wellington, New Zealand (email: judd.ormsby@motu.org.nz)
[3] Motu Economic and Public Policy Research, Wellington, New Zealand (email: anna_robinson@hotmail.com)
[4] University of Auckland, Auckland, New Zealand (email: siuyuat@gmail.com)

Received: 14 January 2016/Accepted: 30 March 2016

Abstract. We study the association between fiscal policy and subjective wellbeing using fiscal data on 35 countries and 130 country-years, combined with over 170,000 people's subjective wellbeing scores. While past research has found that 'distortionary taxes' (e.g. income taxes) are associated with slow growth relative to 'non-distortionary' taxes (GST/VAT), we find that distortionary taxes are associated with higher levels of subjective wellbeing than non-distortionary taxes. This relationship holds when we control for macro-economic variables and country fixed effects. If this relationship is causal, it would offer an explanation as to why governments pursue these policies even when they harm economic growth. We find that richer people's subjective wellbeing is harmed less by indirect taxes than for people with lower incomes, while "unproductive expenditure" is associated with higher wellbeing for the middle class relative to others, possibly reflecting middle class capture. We see little evidence for differential effects of fiscal policy on people living in different sized settlements. Devolving a portion of expenditure to subnational government is associated with higher subjective wellbeing but devolving tax collection to subnational government is associated with monotonically lower subjective wellbeing.

JEL classification: D60, E62, H50, H70, O57

Key words: Subjective wellbeing, Fiscal policy, Decentralized government

1 Introduction

Beginning with Barro (1990), there have been a number of endogenous growth models that attempt to understand the impacts of fiscal policy on both growth and wellbeing. Many researchers have attempted to empirically test the model's predictions for economic growth, but economic growth is only a means to an end – the end being greater wellbeing. Despite

*This research was funded by Marsden Fund grant MEP1201 from the Royal Society of New Zealand. We are grateful for this assistance. We thank seminar participants at the New Zealand Association of Economists conference (July 2015) and the European Regional Science Association conference (September 2015) for their helpful comments. We also thank three anonymous referees as well as Phillip Morrison and Norman Gemmell for their comments on an earlier version. The usual disclaimer applies.

this, far less attention has gone to testing the endogenous growth model's implications for wellbeing. We help to fill this gap by connecting the fiscal policy and growth literature to the subjective wellbeing (SWB) literature.

To the best of our knowledge this study is the first in the SWB literature to explicitly consider the government budget constraint, the first to consider SWB within the context of endogenous growth theory, one of few (including within the growth literature) to use the IMF's higher quality general (rather than central) government fiscal data, and the first to examine regional and subnational dimensions of the relationship of fiscal policies with subjective wellbeing.

While previous literature has argued that 'non-distortionary' indirect (sales) taxes are good for economic growth relative to 'distortionary' taxes, we find that distortionary taxes are associated with relatively higher levels of subjective wellbeing than are non-distortionary taxes. This result is robust to several different specifications. In addition, we find some indication that indirect taxes hurt the poor more than the rich, and we find the opposite relationship for distortionary taxation. As the model of Alesina, Rodrik (1994) predicts, we find evidence that productive expenditures benefit the poor relatively more than the rich. This result is not driven by people's political ideology, supporting the idea that fiscal policies affect wellbeing through effects on the real economy. "Unproductive expenditure" appears to benefit the middle class by more than it benefits the rich or poor, consistent with middle class capture as predicted by the median voter model.

We also study the impacts on subjective wellbeing of devolving government expenditure and taxation to subnational government. We find devolution of taxation is associated with lower subjective wellbeing, while partial devolution of expenditure is associated with higher subjective wellbeing. This is consistent with subnational authorities having better information on their constituents' wants and thus better ability to target resources. Taxation may be more simply administered by central government and the advantages to being better informed by constituents may be outweighed by economies of scale.

We find little variation when we interact fiscal policies with settlement size variables. Thus rural residents apparently have similar subjective wellbeing reactions to alternative fiscal policies as their urban counterparts.

We control for many unobservable and observable factors that affect fiscal policy and subjective wellbeing; importantly we control for country fixed effects, survey wave (i.e. time) fixed effects, personal characteristics, and country-specific, time-varying macroeconomic conditions. Our results can be interpreted causally if, aside from the variables that we already control for (including our macroeconomic controls), there are no other country-specific, time-varying factors that affect both fiscal policy and subjective wellbeing or any reverse causality from subjective wellbeing to fiscal policy. This is known as the parallel trends assumption[1]. We find it plausible that trends are parallel, especially after controlling for macro-economic variables, since we have not identified other country-specific, time-varying omitted factors that would bias our results. There is also no obvious reason why there would be reverse causality. However fiscal policy is chosen by countries (rather than randomly allocated) in part to reflect their changing circumstances, so we cannot completely eliminate the possibility that these decisions depend on some unobserved time-varying, country-specific variables that also affect subjective wellbeing[2]. We leave it to future research to analyze further the causal pathways that may underpin the relationships that we estimate.

Section 2 of the paper reviews the relevant theory. We discuss our data in Section 3, describe our methodology in Section 4, present our results in Section 5, and conclude in Section 6.

---

[1]In any study, even a randomised control trial, the counterfactual – in our case what would have happened to subjective wellbeing in the absence of fiscal policy change – is unobserved and hence the parallel trends assumption can never be directly tested. For a formal treatment of this issue see chapter 2 of Angrist, Pischke (2008).

[2]Clearly a randomised trial is not feasible for fiscal policy research.

2   Theoretical framework

2.1   The Barro framework

Barro (1990) examined the role of fiscal policy within an endogenous growth framework –
extending the previous work of Lucas (1988), Rebelo (1991), Romer (1986, 1988). Barro
sets up a simple infinitely-lived representative agent model with lifetime utility, U, given
by Equation (1).

$$U = \int_0^\infty u_t\left(c_t, h_t\right) e^{-\rho t}\, dt \tag{1}$$

where $\rho > 0$ is the rate of time preference and u_t is instantaneous utility. Crucially
instantaneous utility, u_t, depends on both private consumption, c_t, and government
consumption services h_t. Because h_t enters the utility function directly and not the
production function it has been termed as an unproductive expenditure in the successive literature (e.g. Kneller et al. 1999, Bleaney et al. 2001, Angelopoulos et al. 2007).
In addition to providing consumption services, the government also funds productive
expenditures, g_t, that enter the production function alongside private capital (k_t):

$$y_t = \Phi(k_t, g_t) \tag{2}$$

where y_t is aggregate output. As is standard in endogenous growth theory, Φ exhibits
constant (or increasing) returns to scale. The full detail of the model is spelled out
in Barro (1990). One of Barro's key results is that an increase in the share of output
devoted to unproductive expenditures (h_t/y_t in the notation above) reduces growth of
output, capital and consumption, but potentially increases lifetime utility. As Barro and
Sala-i-Martin put it in a later paper: "An increase in $\left[\frac{h_t}{y_t}\right]$ can be consistent with an
increase in utility that accompanies a decrease in the growth rate" (Barro, Sala-i Martin
1992, 651)[3]. The growth slowdown occurs because the increase in income taxes lowers
the private marginal product of capital, discouraging private investment; however, if the
additional tax revenue is used to provide public services valued by households (h_t), overall
utility may be raised.

The Barro model only includes income taxes and lump sum taxes. Labor supply is
treated as perfectly inelastic and so consumption taxes are equivalent to a lump-sum tax.
This has led to the potentially confusing convention of referring to consumption, sales,
and value-added taxes (i.e. indirect taxes) as non-distortionary taxation in the subsequent
empirical literature – again see, for example, Bleaney et al. (2001), Kneller et al. (1999),
Angelopoulos et al. (2007). With endogenous labor supply, such consumption taxes are
distortionary. With this qualification noted, we will continue with the terminology of
previous authors so as to make our analysis comparable with theirs.

In the Barro model, with a representative agent, the socially optimal outcome cannot be
obtained by income taxation as it distorts private incentives to save. Meanwhile lump-sum
taxes produce a higher level of growth than income taxes but they too can fail to generate
the socially optimal output level, as the optimum requires getting the government size
just right[4]. With heterogeneous agents who value unproductive expenditures differently,
the simple results from this model with regard to fiscal categories may no longer hold.

There have been many extensions to the basic Barro model. Misch et al. (2013)
and also Baier, Glomm (2001) show that optimal fiscal policy depends on the degree
of complementarity between g and k: a high degree of complementarity results in a
larger optimum government size and an optimal growth rate that is lower than the

---

[3]We have modified the notation to match that used above.

[4]Extra government expenditure on g_t always increases each of the private marginal product of capital,
savings and growth. If g_t is financed through distortionary taxation, this acts as a countervailing force
decreasing the private return to capital so that growth first increases and then decreases with g_t. In the
case of lump-sum taxation there is no such countervailing force and so growth increases monotonically in
g_t.

growth-maximizing one[5]. The importance of transitional dynamics is shown both by Baier, Glomm (2001) and Futagami et al. (1993). Turnovsky (2000) adds endogenous labor supply, demonstrating that an equilibrium growth path may not even exist. With endogenous labor-leisure trade-offs, consumption taxes become distortionary unlike in Barro (1990). This additional literature demonstrates that welfare maximizing fiscal policy is complex: the optimal policy setting depends on the exact model and is therefore an empirical question.

One last model, especially relevant to our work, is that of Alesina, Rodrik (1994). Alesina and Rodrik take the Barro framework and introduce variation in people's ownership of capital. In this model, the welfare of a pure capitalist – someone whose income is entirely from capital – is maximized when the growth rate is maximized, but all others prefer higher taxation and lower growth (and the lower their share of capital relative to labor income, the higher taxes they desire). The higher taxes are useful to laborers not through direct cash transfers, but because government-provided capital increases labor productivity. We test – and find some support for – the hypothesis that productive expenditure disproportionally benefits the poor[6].

2.2 Theory meets empirics

Nijkamp, Poot (2004) conducted a meta-analysis of 93 empirical journal articles on the effects of fiscal policies on growth, finding mixed results for these effects. A key problem with many of the early papers that they reviewed is that the papers rarely gave due consideration to the government's budget constraint. For example, papers tested for the effects of taxation without controlling for how revenues are spent, or tested for the effects of government spending without controlling for how the revenues are raised. One exception is Bleaney et al. (2001), whose methodology we adapt for subjective wellbeing. We outline their approach in our methodology section.

2.3 SWB and fiscal policy literature

There is only a small and recent literature on the effects of fiscal policies on subjective wellbeing. The results are mixed. For example, several papers look at the relationship between the size of government consumption and subjective wellbeing. Results include finding a negative relationship (Bjørnskov et al. 2007, Oishi et al. 2011), finding no relationship (Ram 2009), finding a positive relationship (Flavin et al. 2011, 2014), and finding an inverse U pattern (Hessami 2010). Other papers have looked at taxation with Flavin et al. (2011, 2014) finding higher taxation associated with higher SWB. Oishi et al. (2011) find more progressive tax systems are correlated with higher SWB. Veenhoven (2000) examines social security generosity and finds no relationship with SWB.

Most of these papers are cross sectional. Only Flavin et al. (2011, 2014) and Veenhoven (2000) estimate country fixed effects, despite the obvious importance of country effects for both SWB (e.g. through culture) and fiscal policy (again possibly through culture, or through circumstances like natural resource endowments)[7]. None of these papers takes into account the structure of taxation or how government consumption is financed, and none of these papers uses the high quality IMF general government data.

---

[5]This result holds even though Misch et al. (2013) did not include government consumption services, h_t. As Barro had already shown, the presence of these services also leads to a non-maximal optimal growth rate.

[6]One qualification is that our data is on relative income rank rather than capital wealth rank. However, a) higher income is correlated with higher wealth, and b) Alesina and Rodrik state: "When we use the term capital, for example, what we have in mind are all growth-producing assets, including physical capital, human capital, and proprietary technology. Labor, in turn, stands for unskilled labor." (Alesina, Rodrik 1994). In light of a) and b), low-income earners seem to be a reasonable proxy for their unskilled laborers, and high income earners seem a reasonable proxy for their capitalists.

[7]Even here the country panels are short, with Veenhoven (2000) only having two time periods to work with and hence just running a regression on the within country changes in SWB and social security generosity.

2.3.1 SWB validation

SWB has become increasingly recognized as an important area of study as research has validated it as an informative measure of wellbeing. SWB is highly correlated in test-retest comparisons of the same individual a short time apart (e.g. see Diener et al. 2013). While some studies have shown that SWB can be influenced by seemingly arbitrary factors (e.g. Schwarz 1987), on average these vicissitudes will wash out in large samples such as ours. Many studies show a good correlation between SWB and other subjective and objective measures of wellbeing. For example, within a given country those who are richer are more satisfied with their lives, and across countries, developing countries are less satisfied than developed ones. Stevenson, Wolfers (2008) show that these cross-sectional relationships remain robust when considered in a time series context unlike the earlier findings of Easterlin (1974). Stevenson and Wolfers emphasize the log-linear rather than linear nature of the relationship between GDP per capita and SWB. They also emphasize that the positive point estimate for the relationship is robust even if its statistical significance is less so in some subsamples[8]. Helliwell, Huang (2008) show that life satisfaction is closely correlated with many of the World Bank's measures of good government. Di Tella et al. (2003) find that recessions lower SWB. Finally studies in other fields have found evidence that SWB correlates with other measures of people's welfare[9].

Several studies have found differences in rural versus urban SWB (Easterlin et al. 2011, Morrison 2011, Berry, Okulicz-Kozaryn 2011, 2009, Veenhoven 1994)[10]. For these reasons we include controls for settlement size and test whether relationships differ across large versus small settlements.

3 Data

3.1 Fiscal Variables

The majority of our fiscal data is sourced from the IMF Government Finance Statistics database (IMF 2014), supplemented with OECD data where IMF data is missing (OECD 2014). Unlike almost all previous studies (in both the SWB and growth literature), we make use of general government as well as central government data: the former provides us with a more complete picture of a nation's fiscal policy settings, while the latter has better coverage. The use of both datasets together allows us to explore the SWB effects of decentralization of fiscal policy.

Following the Barro model, we split each of expenditure and taxation into two main categories: distortionary and non-distortionary taxation, and productive and unproductive expenditures. We also include two residual categories, "other revenue", OR, and "other expenditure", OE, plus the budget surplus (BS). Our taxonomy is the same as in much of the empirical growth literature; specifically we use the definitions of Bleaney et al. (2001) to make our results for the effects of fiscal policy on SWB directly comparable with their results for the effects on growth. These category definitions are described in detail in Table A.1. Broadly speaking, non-distortionary taxation, NDT, is defined as indirect taxes on goods and services (i.e. GST/VAT), while distortionary taxation, DT, is taxation on income, social security contributions, and property taxes. Productive expenditures, PE, include education, health, housing, transport, defense and general public services. Unproductive expenditures, UE, include social security and welfare, recreation and economic services. Each of these variables is expressed as a percentage of the country's GDP[11]. Summary statistics of these, and other country-level variables, can

---

[8]Easterlin et al. (2010) and Helliwell et al. (2012) are not convinced by these results with the latter pointing to the importance of the countries that are included in the analysis as well as which control variables are included. Clearly the debate is not yet settled.

[9]Studies in psychology have shown links between brain scans known to be associated with happiness and higher SWB (Urry et al. 2004). People who are more satisfied with their lives appear to live longer (Diener, Chan 2011). Early studies showed lower SWB predicted suicide (Helliwell 2007, Daly, Wilson 2009, Daly et al. 2013, Layard 2005), but a recent study by Case, Deaton (2015) found more mixed results.

[10]It appears that in developing countries people are more satisfied living in cities, while in developed countries there appears to be either no difference or the opposite relationship (Grimes, Reinhardt 2015).

[11]We use GDP data from the UN. The UN has several different nominal GDP series available reflecting

be found in Table A.2. More details about our data cleaning process can be found in the Appendix, as well as in our Stata code.

3.2 Subjective wellbeing and personal controls

We use data on subjective wellbeing (SWB) from the World Values Survey (WVSA 2014) and the European Values Survey (EVS 2011). Subjective wellbeing is asked (in the local language) as:

> All things considered, how satisfied are you with your life as a whole these days? Please use this card to help with your answer. 'Dissatisfied' 1 2 3 4 5 6 7 8 9 10 'Satisfied'.

SWB is tightly distributed in all countries. Mean SWB is approximately 7.3 with a standard deviation of approximately 2 across all the individuals in our analysis. Figure A.1 shows the distribution of country means and standard deviations within different country-years,[12] while Figure A.2 provides a histogram of SWB scores. Because of SWB's tight distribution, even numerically small changes in SWB can be economically meaningful. For example Clark et al. (2008, 241) find that marriage increases SWB by about 0.3-0.4 after one year, and the largest shock they studied – widowhood – decreases SWB by about 1 unit. Across OECD countries the standard deviation is about 0.6, with a difference in average SWB of just 0.5 separating the 15th and 5th best position[13].

Both WVS and EVS include information on people's age, gender, education, settlement size, and political orientation. Table A.3 provides summary statistics for key variables. We include age in six categories[14], education in eight categories[15], and settlement size in four categories[16]. Political orientation and income are measured on a 10 point scale, entered in our regressions as categorical variables[17]. For each of these variables we include two extra categories for missing information: missing because the question was not asked in the survey, and missing for other reasons[18]. Finally we include a dummy variable to distinguish between the WVS and the EVS.

Donnelly, Pop-Eleches (2012) criticize the WVS and EVS measures of income. They point out that the income distributions associated with these 10 categories are not usually interpretable as deciles, as some researchers have interpreted them, and that the method used to record income varies. In the vast majority of surveys (210 out of 245), respondents are asked to place themselves in one of 10 income brackets (e.g. $0-$1,000, $1,000–$5000 etc.), where the brackets available were pre-determined by WVS/EVS, though 58 of these countries are missing documentation on the exact brackets used (Donnelly, Pop-Eleches 2012, 3). These brackets often do not generate uniform decile distributions of income. In other cases, respondents are asked to subjectively place themselves on a ten point scale

---

definitional issues and currency changes. Where possible we use one consistent series for each country in the same currency as the fiscal data. When this is not possible, we splice overlapping series to form one longer series.

[12]Figure A.1 should not be interpreted as showing a meaningful correlation between mean SWB in a country and that country's s.d. of SWB. Because SWB is bounded above, a DGP with a high mean will generate a disproportionate number of 10s and thus mechanically have a lower s.d. than a DGP with a mean of 5.

[13]Here we are comparing the (unweighted) average SWB of OECD countries using each country's latest measure of SWB from either the EVS or WVS.

[14]Under 19, 19–24, 25–34, 35–49, 50–64, and 65+.

[15]The categories, as per the world values data labels, are: "Inadequately completed elementary education", "Completed (compulsory) elementary education", "Incomplete secondary school: technical/vocational", "Complete secondary school: technical/vocational" "Incomplete secondary: university-preparation", "Complete secondary: university-preparation" "Some university without degree/Higher education", "University with degree/Higher education".

[16]Less than 5000, 5000–20,000/25,000, 20,000/25,000–100,000 and 100,000+. The reason for the blur between town populations of 20 and 25 thousand is because of changing survey definitions over time. Settlements in that interval are included in one category or the other, not both.

[17]In 1982 in the United States income was put on an 11 point scale, with 102 people coded as 11. We recode these people as 10.

[18]In practice it is common for several question to be omitted at once, so in these cases we cannot estimate separate coefficients for each missing category due to perfect multicollinearity among these categories. In this case only one coefficient is estimated capturing missing responses.

where 1 represents the first decile and 10 the highest. In such cases, most people respond with a middle number: for example 84% of Americans in the 2006 wave claim they are in one of the middle 5 deciles (deciles 3-7). Finally in some cases respondents are asked to write down their income, whereby WVS/EVS later recode it onto a ten point scale, in some cases to match pre-determined brackets, in other cases to perfectly split the data into ten equally populated deciles.

Because of these survey inconsistencies we interpret income purely as an ordinal variable within a given country year: i.e. if somebody is on a higher income step than someone else in the same country-year they likely earn more, but we do not know the cardinal relationships between categories.

3.3 Macroeconomic controls

In most specifications we include controls for real PPP-adjusted GDP per capita (current and lagged three years), unemployment, investment, and inflation. We calculate real GDP per capita as real PPP-adjusted GDP divided by population, with both figures coming from the Penn World Tables, version 8.1 (Feenstra et al. 2015) except in the case of 2012 data, where we use data from the World Bank (The World Bank 2015b)[19]. Our primary source of data on unemployment is from the Annual Macro Economics Database (European Commission 2015). For countries where we do not have AMECO data we use the World Bank development indicators data, (The World Bank 2015c) spliced, where necessary, with UN unemployment data (The United Nations 2015)[20]. We source inflation data for all but three countries from the World Bank development indicators[21]. All investment data is from the World Bank development indicators (The World Bank 2015b,c)[22]. Table A.4 lists the countries used in each of our regressions.

4 Methodology

Equation (3) illustrates our baseline equation. We estimate subjective wellbeing for individual i in country c at time t as a function of our fiscal variables, $\boldsymbol{F}$, a vector of personal controls, $\boldsymbol{X}$, a vector of macro controls, $\boldsymbol{M}$, country fixed effects, λ_c, and survey wave (time) fixed effects, λ_w.

$$SWB_{i,c,t} = \beta_0 + \boldsymbol{\beta_F F} + \beta_2 \boldsymbol{X} + \beta_3 \boldsymbol{M} + \lambda_w + \lambda_c + \epsilon \tag{3}$$
where
$$\boldsymbol{\beta_F F} = \beta_{NDT} NDT + \beta_{DT} DT + \beta_{PE} PE + \beta_{UE} UE + \beta_{OR} OR + \beta_{OE} OE$$

with the budget surplus BS omitted to avoid perfect multicollinearity. In other specifications we make some modifications to Equation (3), e.g. removing the macro controls, including an interaction of our fiscal variables with income and political affiliation, and including the proportion of each fiscal category which is spent subnationally.

Our analysis includes countries only if we observe them in more than one year. This allows us to estimate country fixed effects λ_c. Researchers have worried about whether the SWB question is understood the same way across different countries. Separately,

---

[19]This is because the Penn World Tables v8.1 do not extend to 2012. The World Bank data is spliced multiplicatively with the PWT data.

[20]The splicing occurs when the World Bank data do not go back far enough. The splicing method we use here differs from the multiplicative method we use to splice GDP together. For unemployment our splice method is: First, find the first year the World Bank and United Nation's series overlap. Second, calculate the difference between these two series at this point, denoted U_WB-U_UN. Third, for all points earlier than this overlap, where World Bank data is missing, we define unemployment to be the United Nations rate plus U_WB-U_UN.

[21]We use OECD inflation data for Chile and the United Kingdom, and we use FRED data (which is itself originally from the World Bank) for Argentina, accessed on 10 November 2015 (The World Bank 2015a).

[22]The investment data ("Gross capital formation as percent of GDP" series code = ne.gdi.totl.zs) is the 14th of October 2015 version of the World Bank development indicators (accessed on the 12th of November 2015), except for Lithuania, where we use the 14 April 2015 release of the indicators (accessed 26 June 2015) because the October release does not include data for Lithuania prior to 2004.

different cultures may have different average levels of subjective wellbeing. In both cases, failure to control for these could bias our estimate of β_F. Country fixed effects allow us to control for, among other things, constant cultural effects over time[23].

In addition to country fixed effects, we control for survey wave fixed effects, λ_w. The survey waves are: 1981-84, 1989-93, 1994-98, 1999-04, 2005-09, 2010-12[24]. These are important as they allow us to control for any changes in survey practices across survey wave. For example the order of question and types of questions elsewhere in the survey can change, possibly affecting people's responses. The wave fixed effects will also pick up global shocks to macro and other variables (for example global recessions such as the global financial crisis which may affect both SWB and our fiscal variables).

The government's budget constraint requires that in each year all taxes be spent or saved, and that all expenditure be funded by taxation or borrowing. Formally:

$$DT_t + NDT_t + OR_t = PE_t + UE_t + OE_t + BS_t \qquad (4)$$

As Bleaney et al. (2001) emphasize, it is vital to recognise the government's budget constraint when analysing the effects of fiscal policy. Fiscal policy does not occur in a vacuum: expenditure must be financed, and taxes must be spent or saved. If one looks at a variable in isolation, say productive expenditure, then one cannot obtain a clear picture of its impact on wellbeing because its effect on wellbeing will depend on whether it is funded from reducing unproductive expenditures, increasing distortionary or non-distortionary taxes, or by borrowing the funds.

Because of the perfect collinearity described in Equation (4) one category must be omitted when we estimate Equation (3). The coefficients on each fiscal variable are then interpreted as the effect of increasing that variable by one unit financed by changing the omitted category. In our regressions we omit the budget surplus, so that for an increase in an expenditure variable the assumption is that the surplus is reduced, while for taxation variables the assumption is that the surplus is increased.

After estimating Equation (3) with the surplus omitted, it is trivial to compute the associations relative to an alternative financing assumption. One simply adds or subtracts the coefficients estimated in Equation (3); for example, to find the effect of increasing PE by one percent of GDP funded by increasing DT one should add $\widehat{\beta_{PE}}$ and $\widehat{\beta_{DT}}$. If the increase in PE were instead funded by reducing UE, then one should subtract $\widehat{\beta_{UE}}$ from $\widehat{\beta_{PE}}$.

The effects of fiscal policies could be nonlinear. For example, perhaps a small amount of non-distortionary taxation is beneficial for SWB, while too much is detrimental. One way of dealing with such nonlinearities would be to include polynomials into the specification. However, given the complication of the government's budget constraint, marginal effects would then become difficult to interpret. Whether, say, more distortionary taxation funded from a reduction in non-distortionary taxation was beneficial for SWB would depend on the existing amount of *both* distortionary and non-distortionary taxation. In addition to the issues of interpretation, we are wary of overfitting the model, and picking up outliers, if we were to estimate such nonlinearities. The same problems present themselves for the fiscal policy and growth literature (discussed above) and we are not aware of papers that deal with both the government's budget constraint and nonlinearities in fiscal policy. Given the difficulties in adequately dealing with these issues we leave analysis of the impacts of such nonlinearities for separate research.

All our equations are estimated using OLS with two-way fixed effects and a suite of personal and macroeconomic controls. As discussed above, fiscal policies are chosen, rather than being randomly assigned. One can think of isolated cases where a shock to most individuals' wellbeing is correlated with shocks to one or more fiscal variables. For instance, even in the absence of any macroeconomic effects, a terrorist attack may lower SWB while raising defense expenditure. Intuitively, however, such examples appear to be isolated, especially once any conduits through macroeconomic conditions are controlled for.

---

[23]Other factors controlled for by fixed effects include, inter alia, climate and geography.

[24]We prefer wave effects (i.e. groups of years) to the finer grained year effects as we sometimes only observe one or two countries' SWB in a given year. Including year effects would effectively remove these observations from our analysis.

At a practical level randomization of fiscal policy is off the table, and suitable instruments for fiscal policy variables are hard to come by since most variables that are correlated with fiscal policy could also directly affect SWB. Even if one could find instruments that satisfy the exclusion restriction, they would need to be strong, and no strong instruments present themselves. While our study is at least as well identified as the fiscal policy and growth literature, we still speak of associations or relationships rather than causal connections because we cannot definitively rule out violations of parallel trends.

5 Results

As emphasized in the previous section, when estimating the effects of fiscal categories on wellbeing (or growth), none of the fiscal coefficients can be interpreted in isolation. To aid comparisons of coefficients with each other, we plot the estimated coefficients graphically together with their 90% confidence intervals. Detailed regression tables for Figure 1 and Figure 5 can be found in the appendix[25].

5.1 Baseline Results

Figure 1 plots the coefficients from four different regressions. The top set of results (i.e. the first four listed fiscal categories) uses the general government data as our fiscal variables, F, whilst the bottom set of results use the central government data. A coefficient of zero implies that an increase in that variable has the same effect on SWB as the omitted category – the surplus. For each regression, we present results without macroeconomic controls (the upper of each pair) and with the inclusion of macroeconomic controls to show whether results are sensitive to their inclusion. All regressions contain the controls for personal characteristics.

In all four regressions, distortionary taxes are associated with higher subjective wellbeing than non-distortionary taxation, and productive expenditures are associated with higher subjective wellbeing than unproductive expenditures. Adding macro controls makes very little difference to the results: non-distortionary taxation appears to be worse for SWB when macro controls are added to the general government regression, but the effect is imprecisely estimated (as evidenced by the wide confidence intervals), and the point estimate hardly changes when macro controls are added to the central government regression.

The magnitude of the coefficients shows the SWB effect of a 1 percentage point-sized change in the fiscal variable (funded by changing the surplus) as a proportion of GDP. The differences between different tax and expenditure estimates are economically meaningful. For example, reducing distortionary taxation by 10 percent of GDP funded by a same sized rise in non-distortionary taxation is associated with an approximate 0.6 unit rise in SWB, about 25% of a standard deviation. This effect is larger than the (transitory) effect of getting married found in Clark et al. (2008), and it is enough to move a country's subjective wellbeing rank from around 15th out of the 34 OECD countries to about 5th.

5.2 Differential effects of fiscal policy

We examine whether the impacts of fiscal policy on SWB vary according to income and political persuasion. Noting the similarity of results above using central and general government definitions, and given the larger sample size afforded by the central government dataset, we estimate these equations based on the central government data. All results in this section include all macro and personal controls.

5.2.1 Income

With progressive income taxes, higher income earners pay a higher percentage of their income in income tax than low income earners, while under consumption taxes poorer people pay a higher percentage of their income than high income earners (assuming that

---

[25] The non-parametric estimates in Figures 2-4 have too many coefficients to be usefully presented in a table; the coefficients and p-values for the linear interaction terms are shown within the figures.

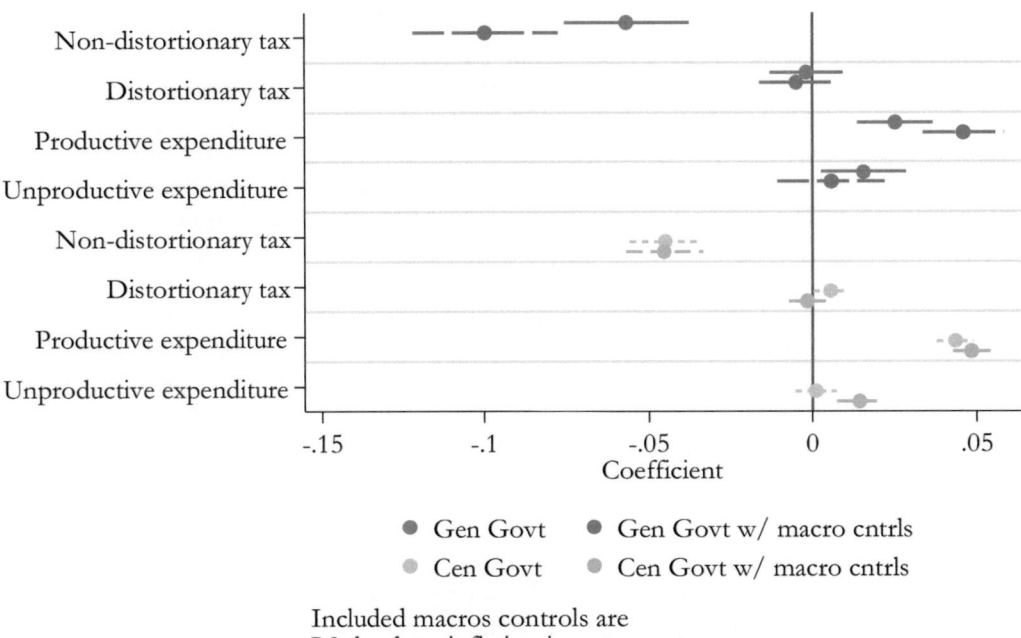

Figure 1: Baseline estimates (90% CI)

poorer people save less). Given these differences in incidence, we explore whether people at different parts of the income spectrum have different SWB responses to the various fiscal categories.

We examine these effects in two ways. First, we treat income as a continuous variable and interact it linearly with each fiscal category. Second, we treat income as a categorical variable and interact each income category with each of the four main fiscal policies $\boldsymbol{F}_M$ as in equation (5):[26]

$$SWB_{i,c,t} = \beta_0 + \beta_2 \boldsymbol{X} + \beta_3 \boldsymbol{M} + \lambda_w + \lambda_c + \lambda_{inc} + \beta_F \boldsymbol{F} + \beta_{int}(\lambda_{inc} \times \boldsymbol{F}_M) + \epsilon \quad (5)$$

This non-parametric approach does not impose any functional form assumption, but has the drawback of decreasing the precision of our estimates.

Figure 2 plots the marginal effects of our fiscal variables from both specifications across the ten income ranks[27]. The dashed lines present the marginal effects of the linearly interacted variable, with the slope estimate and its associated p-value displayed beneath each graph. The solid line links the non-parametric estimates (with associated 90% confidence intervals). As expected, our results indicate that distortionary taxation has a more negative effect for higher income earners, and non-distortionary taxation has a more negative effect on lower income earners. Productive expenditure also appears to be favored by poorer individuals, consistent with Alesina, Rodrik (1994), where productive expenditure especially improves the welfare of unskilled laborers (see Section 2).

The results for unproductive expenditures, which mainly comprises social welfare spending, is found to have most benefit for the middle class and least benefit for poorer people. Indeed, the point estimate for the poorest people is negative. This result is consistent with middle class capture, as in median voter models[28]. An alternative explanation is that this result could reflect the countercyclical nature of unproductive expenditures combined with an assumption that business cycles affect the poor the most

---

[26] Recall, as discussed in Section 3.2, that our income variable is an ordinal measure of a person's relative income within the country and year that they were surveyed.

[27] The omitted category is again the surplus. We do not interact the (residual) other revenue or other expenditure categories, though we do continue to include them as controls without interactions.

[28] In median voter models the median voter determines policy. See Hotelling (1929), Black (1948), and Bowen (1943) for the original papers developing the theory. See the section on majority voting in chapter 6 of Stiglitz (1988) for a modern textbook introduction.

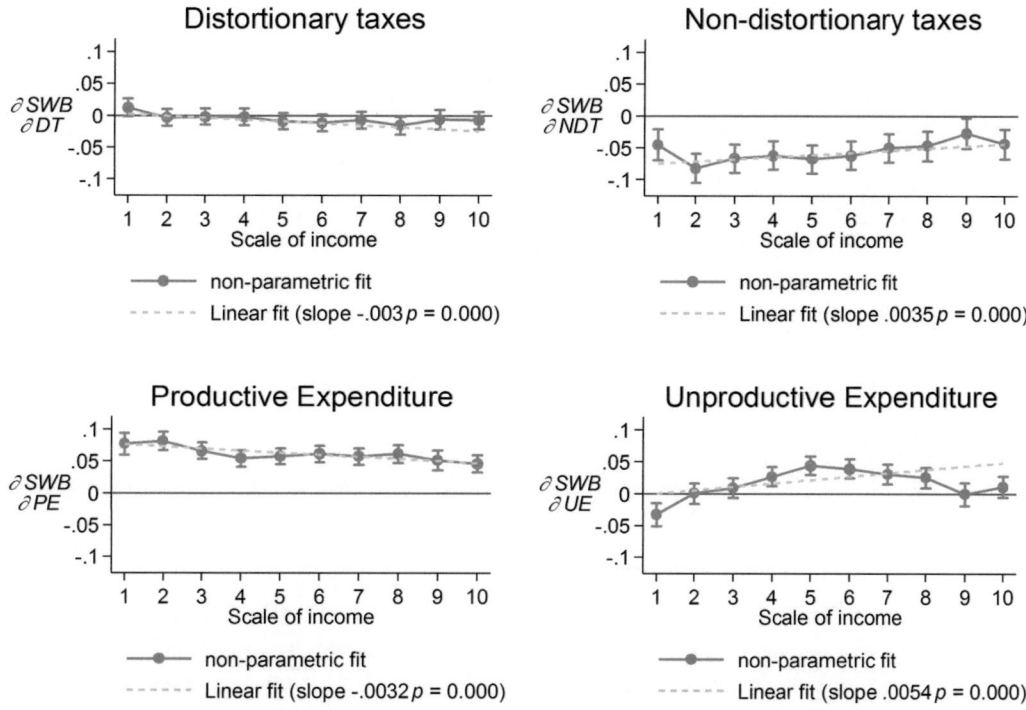

Figure 2: Marginal effects by income group (90% CI)

and the middle class the least. To minimize this potential source of bias, our estimates include controls for unemployment, investment, inflation, current GDP and lagged GDP, so this alternative explanation would require that these variables do not sufficiently control for the business cycle.

5.2.2   Political orientation

It is possible that fiscal policy affects utility directly through political preferences (ideologies) instead of through the fiscal policy's influence on the real economy (h and c). We examine whether this may be the case. If such a phenomenon were driving our results, we would expect to see different effects of fiscal policy depending on political orientation. We repeat the same interaction procedures as described above for income, but replacing income with people's political orientation. As can be seen from Figure 3, we find the same effect of fiscal policies for people of different political orientations: the slope estimates are smaller than for the income interactions and none are significant at the 5% level (though the interaction with distortionary taxation is significant at the 10% level), while the non-parametric fits reveal no discernible trend.

5.3   Regions: Heterogeneous settlement size and subnational effects

Our prior results all control for the settlement size of the individual respondent but do not allow the fiscal impacts to vary by settlement size, nor do they test whether national versus subnational fiscal policies have differential effects on SWB. In addition, fiscal policy may affect wealthier countries differently to less wealthy ones and this effect may differ by town size. Here we test each of these region-related aspects.

5.3.1   Settlement size and country income

We investigate whether fiscal policies affect people living in different sized towns and cities in different ways. To do so, we interact the size of a person's settlement with the fiscal policy variables. We test whether these effects may differ according to the wealth of countries by creating a dummy variable (richer/poorer), which splits our sample roughly in half, based on 1990 GDP per capita (using PWT 8.1 definitions of GDP and

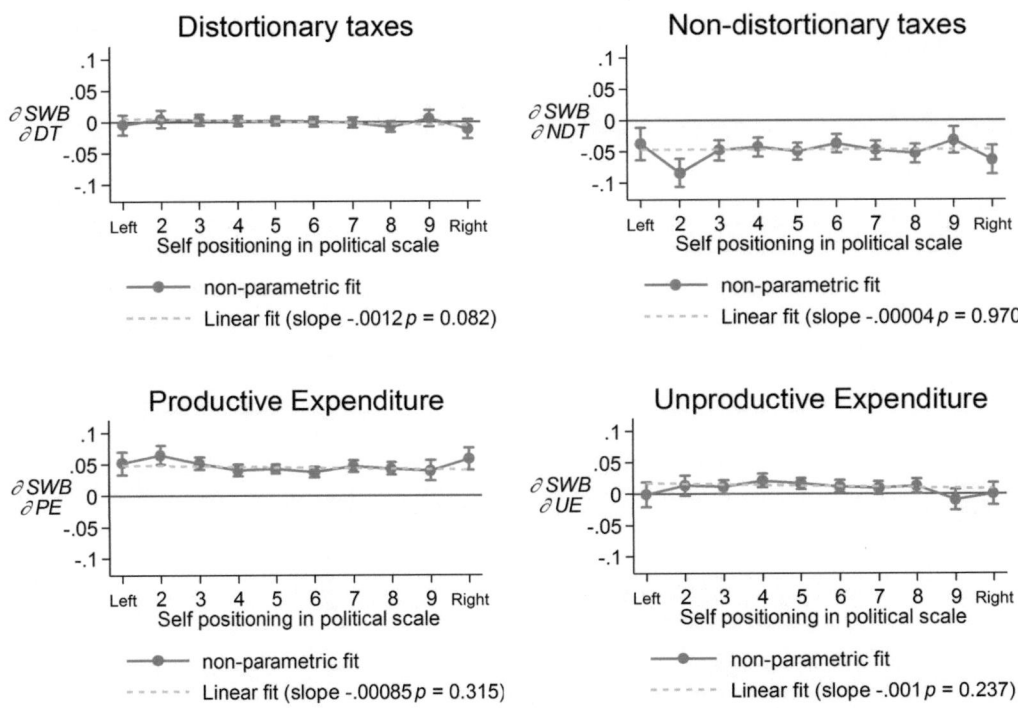

Figure 3: Marginal effects by self-expressed political orientation (90% CI)

population). We stress here that our sample does not include developing countries, and that generally the 'poorer' countries are at least middle income[29]. We then interact our rich/poor variable with both fiscal policy and town size. This allows the effect of each fiscal variable to differ across the 8 different combinations of country wealth and town size.

The results (again using the central government definitions) are presented in Figure 4. (Linear interactions are not included given the non-linear definitions of settlement size in the data.)

Productive expenditure appears to be more beneficial for SWB in poorer countries, while there is some evidence that non-distortionary taxes are more detrimental in poorer countries. Distortionary taxation appears to have similar effects in both rich and poor countries. Unproductive expenditures have a similar effect on SWB in both rich and poor countries, with only weak evidence for more positive effects in richer countries.

Turning to differences in fiscal policy's influence across town size (i.e. the slope of the lines in Figure 4) we find little variation, with the 90% confidence intervals largely overlapping. There is, perhaps, some evidence for differences in effects of distortionary taxes, and productive expenditure in cities with more than 100,000 people ('large cities'), but care should be taken here for several reasons. Firstly, the results differ for wealthier and less wealthy countries; in richer countries the effects of productive expenditure deteriorate in the larger settlements, while in poorer countries the effects of productive expenditure improve in larger settlements. *A priori*, we have no strong reason to suppose this. Relatedly, given the multiple comparisons being made here, deviations like this may occur from chance alone (i.e. a false positive). Finally, the relative incomes of people within a country (rather than the across country differences) are correlated with settlement size, so it is possible that the estimated association found here is driven not by the size of the town *per se* but by the differences in incomes of the people living in these towns.

---

[29]'Poorer' countries in our sample are: Chile, Cyprus, Czech Republic, Estonia, Greece, Hungary, Ireland, Lithuania, Malta, Poland, Portugal, Slovenia, Spain, and the Ukraine. Richer countries in our sample are: Australia, Austria, Belgium, Canada, Denmark, Finland, France, Germany, Italy, Luxembourg, Netherlands, Norway, Sweden, Switzerland, United Kingdom, and the United States.

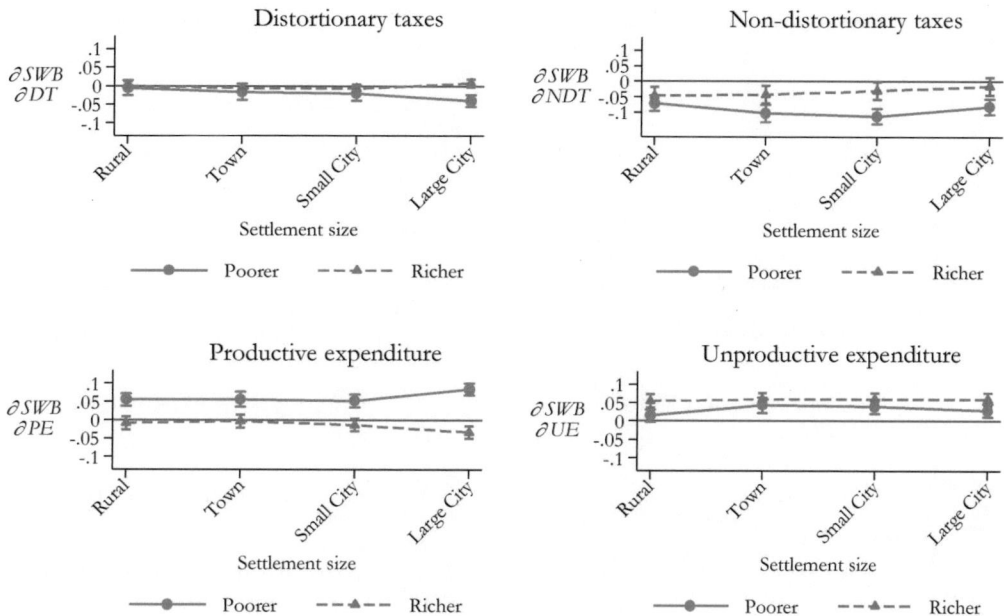

Figure 4: Marginal effects by settlement size and richer/poorer countries (90% CI)

5.3.2 Devolution of fiscal policy to subnational government

We examine the relationship to wellbeing of differences in the degree to which fiscal expenditures and revenues are centralized or decentralized to subnational government. Subnational government is taken to comprise all levels of government below central government (i.e. including both state and municipal governments).

For each fiscal category, we calculated the proportion of general government taxation or expenditure that occurs at the subnational level. The proportion that is subnational is defined as $1 - \frac{var_{CG}}{var_{GG}}$, where var_{CG} is the amount of the fiscal variable reported at the central government level and var_{GG} the amount reported at the general government level. We investigated other definitions but consider this definition to be the most reliable of those available. For example, we had measures of local and regional government fiscal variables from an alternative data source, which we added to form an estimate of the subnational component, var_{SN}, allowing us to estimate the proportion subnational as $\frac{var_{SN}}{var_{CG} + var_{SN}}$ for each fiscal variable. Unfortunately, these estimates of subnational government were often implausible (most probably due to double counting of taxes and expenditures in the subnational categories) and, as a result, the corresponding results differ to those presented below[30]. The measure of subnational government that we use has deficiencies as a result of drawing data from different sources that may have slightly different fiscal definitions to each other (and which could include some double counting), explaining why we have isolated country examples where central government is greater than general government within a particular fiscal category. For these reasons, while we have used the best available data, our results in this section should be interpreted with some caution.

We estimated Equation (6), being our baseline equation modified to include terms for the proportion of each variable that is subnational (denoted by the vector $\boldsymbol{S}$). A non-linear relationship is implied if the optimal level of subnational government is neither 0% nor 100%. We find that a cubic specification best fits the data[31]. Hence, our baseline

---

[30] Our definition of subnational government, $var_{SN} = 1 - \frac{var_{CG}}{var_{GG}}$, could also be affected by double counting in the central government variable (i.e var_{CG} is overestimated due to part of var_{CG} truly being subnational). To the extent this is the case it means our estimate of subnational government is too low, and hence our coefficients on var_{SN} too large in absolute magnitude.

[31] In addition to the cubic specification we estimated the equation with a quadratic specification, as well as linearly. The Akaike criterion, Bayesian information criterion, and adjusted R-square all preferred the cubic specification (see Table A.6). All of the cubic terms were significant at the 1% level except for the coefficient on subnational non-distortionary tax, which was significant at the 10% level.

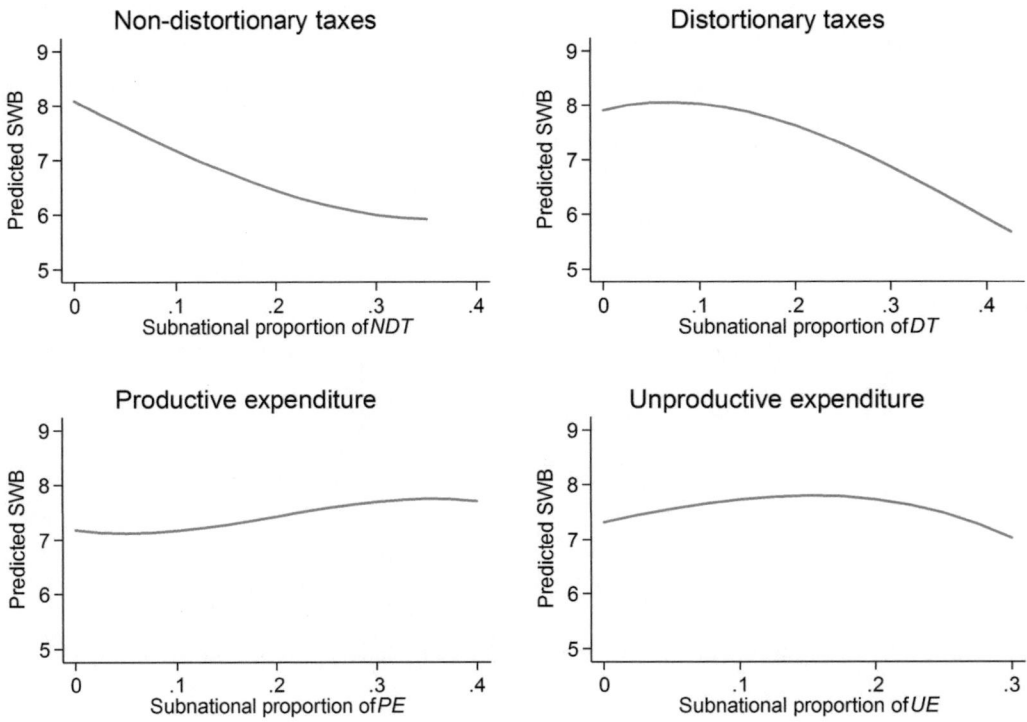

Figure 5: Predicted effects of varying subnational fiscal proportions

estimation includes S^2 and S^3, vectors whose elements are the squares and cubes of the elements in S.

$$SWB_{i,c,t} = \beta_0 + \beta_1 F + \alpha_1 S + \alpha_2 S^2 + \alpha_3 S^3 + \beta_2 X + \beta_3 M + \lambda_w + \lambda_c + \epsilon \quad (6)$$

Figure 5 plots the predicted values from the regression in (6), as each subnational proportion variable is varied between 0 and its 90th percentile in the regression sample. For each plot, all other variables are evaluated at their sample means.

The results suggest that taxation is best done centrally, while expenditure is best done by a combination of central and subnational government. This is consistent with economies of scale being important for revenue raising, and with local knowledge being important for expenditure. In other words, it appears optimal to keep taxation systems simple and centralized, and to allow fiscal expenditures some latitude to reflect local complexities.

6 Conclusions

Economic growth is not an end in itself, but instead is a means to greater utility or wellbeing. While the empirical literature on the effects of fiscal policy has hitherto focussed on GDP growth, we have focused on subjective wellbeing – an important measure of people's overall wellbeing. Our evidence on the relationships between fiscal policy and subjective wellbeing can feed into the decisions of policymakers who have policy goals that extend beyond economic growth.

The small amount of prior literature relating to fiscal policy and wellbeing has focused on the overall size of government, without addressing how government is financed. We adapt the methodology used in the (Bleaney et al. 2001) GDP growth study to explicitly control for the government budget constraint, estimating the relationship between wellbeing and taxation and expenditure shares. In line with the Barro endogenous growth framework and the approach taken by Bleaney, Gemmell and Kneller, we distinguish between the effects of four broad fiscal categories: "productive expenditure", or government-provided capital; "unproductive expenditure", or government-provided consumption; "distortionary taxation" such as income taxes and social security contributions; and "non-distortionary taxation" such as VAT. We retain their definitions of these variables to enable comparisons with the prior literature. This study is, to the best of our knowledge, the first in the SWB literature to explicitly consider the government budget constraint, the first to consider SWB within the context of endogenous growth theory, and the first to examine regional and subnational dimensions of the relationship of fiscal policies with subjective wellbeing.

We use fiscal data from the IMF Government Finance Statistics and the OECD, for 35 countries and 130 country-years. Unlike almost all previous studies, we make use of general government as well as central government data. We combine our fiscal data with over 170,000 individual responses from the World Values Survey and European Values Study and with macroeconomic data from various sources.

We find a number of important relationships, even after including country fixed effects and a suite of macroeconomic and personal controls. First, we find a positive association between SWB and a decrease in non-distortionary taxes funded by an increase in distortionary taxation. Second, we find a positive association between SWB and an increase in productive expenditures funded by a decrease in unproductive expenditures. While we find no material differences across the political spectrum, we do find differences in associations across people of different incomes: Richer people are hurt more by distortionary taxation and less by non-distortionary taxation than poorer people. They also benefit by less than poorer people do from productive expenditures. The middle class appear to benefit the most from unproductive expenditures, consistent with a theory of middle class capture.

In examining regional issues, we find no material differences in the effects of fiscal policy across people living in different-sized settlements. However, we do uncover important patterns related to subnational versus central government fiscal policies. Most notably, we find a positive association, up to a point, between SWB and an increase in the share of expenditures that are spent subnationally. Additionally, we find a negative association between SWB and an increase in the share of tax revenue raised subnationally. Thus our findings support taxation being a central government function while fiscal expenditures appear to be best provided by a combination of central and subnational governments.

Our estimates control for personal characteristics of the over 170,000 individuals in our sample and control for a suite of macroeconomic circumstances that could independently affect wellbeing. We see no strong reason to expect material reverse causality from subjective wellbeing to fiscal policies or to expect any major sources of omitted variables bias, especially given that we have controlled for macroeconomic conditions. Nevertheless, future research could further examine the extent to which the relationships that we establish are causal and examine the causal pathways through which these relationships act. In particular, our findings regarding the optimal roles for subnational versus central government fiscal policies could prove a fruitful area for further research with an emphasis on uncovering particular categories of expenditures (and taxes) that are best retained at the central government level and those that are best devolved to subnational government.

References

Alesina A, Rodrik D (1994) Distributive politics and economic growth. *The Quarterly Journal of Economics* 109: 465–490. CrossRef.

Angelopoulos K, Economides G, Kammas P (2007) Tax-spending policies and economic growth: Theoretical predictions and evidence from the oecd. *European Journal of Political Economy* 23: 885–902. CrossRef.

Angrist JD, Pischke JS (2008) *Mostly Harmless Econometrics: An Empiricist's Companion*. Princeton University Press, Princeton

Baier SL, Glomm G (2001) Long-run growth and welfare effects of public policies with distortionary taxation. *Journal of Economic Dynamics and Control* 25: 2007–2042. CrossRef.

Barro RJ (1990) Government spending in a simple model of endogeneous growth. *Journal of Political Economy* 98: S103–S125. CrossRef.

Barro RJ, Sala-i Martin X (1992) Public finance in models of economic growth. *The Review of Economic Studies* 59: 645–661. CrossRef.

Berry BJL, Okulicz-Kozaryn A (2009) Dissatisfaction with city life: A new look at some old questions. *Cities* 26: 117–124. CrossRef.

Berry BJL, Okulicz-Kozaryn A (2011) An urban-rural happiness gradient. *Urban Geography* 32: 871–883. CrossRef.

Bjørnskov C, Dreher A, Fischer JAV (2007) The bigger the better? Evidence of the effect of government size on life satisfaction around the world. *Public Choice* 130: 267–292. CrossRef.

Black D (1948) On the rationale of group decision-making. *Journal of Political Economy* 56: 23–34. CrossRef.

Bleaney M, Gemmell N, Kneller R (2001) Testing the endogenous growth model: Public expenditure, taxation, and growth over the long run. *Canadian Journal of Economics* 34: 36–57. CrossRef.

Bowen HR (1943) The interpretation of voting in the allocation of economic resources. *The Quarterly Journal of Economics* 58: 27–48. CrossRef.

Case A, Deaton A (2015) Suicide, age, and wellbeing: An empirical investigation. Working paper 21279. National Bureau of Economic Research. http://www.nber.org/papers/w21279. CrossRef.

Clark AE, Diener E, Georgellis Y, Lucas RE (2008) Lags and leads in life satisfaction: A test of the baseline hypothesis. *Economic Journal* 118: F222–F243. CrossRef.

Daly MC, Wilson DJ (2009) Happiness, unhappiness, and suicide: An empirical assessment. *Journal of the European Economic Association* 7: 539–549. CrossRef.

Daly MC, Wilson DJ, Johnson NJ (2013) Relative status and well-being: Evidence from us suicide deaths. *Review of Economics and Statistics* 95: 1480–1500. CrossRef.

Di Tella R, MacCulloch RJ, Oswald AJ (2003) The macroeconomics of happiness. *Review of Economics and Statistics* 85: 809–827. CrossRef.

Diener E, Chan MY (2011) Happy people live longer: Subjective well-being contributes to health and longevity. *Applied Psychology: Health and Well-Being* 3: 1–43. CrossRef.

Diener E, Inglehart R, Tay L (2013) Theory and validity of life satisfaction scales. *Social Indicators Research* 112: 497–527. CrossRef.

Donnelly M, Pop-Eleches G (2012) The questionable validity of income measures in the world values survey. prepared for the princeton university political methodology seminar. http://www.princeton.edu/politics/about/filerepositpry/public/DonnellyPopElechesMarch16.pdf

Easterlin RA (1974) Does economic growth improve the human lot? In: David PA, Reder MW (eds), *Nations and Households in Economic Growth: Essays in Honor of Moses Abramovitz*. Academic Press, New York, 89–125

Easterlin RA, Angelescu L, Zweig JS (2011) The impact of modern economic growth on urban-rural differences in subjective well-being. *World Development* 39: 2187–2198. CrossRef.

Easterlin RA, Angelescu McVey L, Switek M, Sawangfa O, Zweig JS (2010) The happiness–income paradox revisited. *Proceedings of the National Academy of Sciences* 107: 22463–22468. CrossRef.

European Commission (2015) Economic and financial affairs. http://ec.europa.eu/economy_finance/ameco/user/serie/SelectSerie.cfm

EVS – European Values Study (2011) European values study longitudinal data file 1981-2008. Za4804 version 2.0.0. cologne: Gesis. https://dbk.gesis.org/dbksearch/sdesc2.asp?.no=4804&db=e&doi=10.4232/1.11005

Feenstra RC, Inklaar R, Timmer MP (2015) The next generation of the Penn World Table. *American Economic Review* 105: 3150–3182. CrossRef.

Flavin P, Pacek AC, Radcliff B (2011) State intervention and subjective well-being in advanced industrial democracies. *Politics & Policy* 39: 251–269

Flavin P, Pacek AC, Radcliff B (2014) Assessing the impact of the size and scope of government on human well-being. *Social Forces* 92: 1241–1258. CrossRef.

Futagami K, Shibata A, Morita Y (1993) Dynamic analysis of an endogenous growth model with public capital. *The Scandinavian Journal of Economics* 95: 607–625. CrossRef.

Grimes A, Reinhardt MG (2015) Relative income and subjective wellbeing: Intra-national and inter-national comparisons by settlement and country type. Working paper 15-10, Motu Economic and Public Policy Research

Helliwell JF (2007) Well-being and social capital: Does suicide pose a puzzle? *Social Indicators Research* 81: 455–496. CrossRef.

Helliwell JF, Huang H (2008) How's your government? international evidence linking good government and well-being. *British Journal of Political Science* 38: 595–619. CrossRef.

Helliwell JF, Layard R, Sachs J (2012) World happiness report 2012. http://worldhappiness.report/wp-content/uploads/sites/2/2012/04/World_Happiness_Report_2012.pdf

Hessami Z (2010) The size and composition of government spending in europe and its impact on well-being. *Kyklos* 63: 346–382. CrossRef.

Hotelling H (1929) Stability in competition. *The Economic Journal* 39: 41–57. CrossRef.

IMF – International, Monetary Fund (2014) Government finance statistics. http://www.imf.org/external/Pubs/FT/GFS/Manual/2014/gfsfinal.pdf

Kneller R, Bleaney MF, Gemmell N (1999) Fiscal policy and growth: Evidence from oecd countries. *Journal of Public Economics* 74: 171–190. CrossRef.

Layard R (2005) *Happiness: Lessons Form a New Science*. Allen Lane, London

Lucas RE (1988) On the mechanics of economic development. *Journal of Monetary Economics* 22: 3–42. CrossRef.

Misch F, Gemmell N, Kneller R (2013) Growth and welfare maximization in models of public finance and endogenous growth. *Journal of Public Economic Theory* 15: 939–967. CrossRef.

Morrison PS (2011) Local expressions of subjective well-being: The New Zealand experience. *Regional Studies* 45: 1039–1058. CrossRef.

Nijkamp P, Poot J (2004) Meta-analysis of the effect of fiscal policies on long-run growth. *European Journal of Political Economy* 20: 91–124. CrossRef.

OECD (2014) OECD government finance statistics. http://www.oecd-ilibrary.org/economics/data/general-government-accounts_na-gga-data-en

Oishi S, Schimmack U, Diener E (2011) Progressive taxation and the subjective well-being of nations. *Psychological Science* 23: 86–92. CrossRef.

Ram R (2009) Government spending and happiness of the population: Additional evidence from large cross-country samples. *Public Choice* 138: 483–490. CrossRef.

Rebelo S (1991) Long-run policy analysis and long-run growth. *The Journal of Political Economy* 99: 500–521. CrossRef.

Romer PM (1986) Increasing returns and long-run growth. *The Journal of Political Economy* 94: 1002–1037. CrossRef.

Romer PM (1988) Capital accumulation in the theory of long run growth. University of Rochester-Center for Economic Research (RCER). http://ideas.repec.org/p/roc/rocher/123.html

Schwarz N (1987) *Stimmung als Information: Untersuchungen zum Einfluss von Stimmungen auf die Bewertung des eigenen Lebens.* Springer Verlag, Heidelberg. CrossRef.

Stevenson B, Wolfers J (2008) Economic growth and subjective well-being: Reassessing the Easterlin Paradox. National Bureau of Economic Research, http://www.nber.org/papers/w14282. CrossRef.

Stiglitz JE (1988) *Economics of the Public Sector* (Second ed.). W W Norton & Company Inc, New York

The United Nations (2015) UN data. http://data.un.org/

The World Bank (2015a) Consumer price index for Argentina. FRED, Federal Reserve Bank of St. Louis, https://research.stlouisfed.org/fred2/series/DDOE01ARA086NWDB/

The World Bank (2015b) World bank development indicators 2014. The World Bank, http://data.worldbank.org/indicator/NE.GDI.TOTL.ZS

The World Bank (2015c) World bank development indicators 2015. The World Bank

Turnovsky SJ (2000) Fiscal policy, elastic labor supply, and endogenous growth. *Journal of Monetary Economics* 45: 185–210. CrossRef.

Urry HL, Nitschke JB, Dolski I, Jackson DC, Dalton KM, Mueller CJ, Rosenkranz MA, Ryff CD, Singer BH, Davidson RJ (2004) Making a life worth living. Neural correlates of well-being. *Psychological Science* 15: 367–372. CrossRef.

Veenhoven R (1994) How satisfying is rural life? fact and value. In: Cecora J (ed), *Changing Values and Attitudes in Family Households, Implications for Institutional Transition in East and West.* Society for agricultural policy research in rural society, Bonn, Germany, 41–51

Veenhoven R (2000) Well-being in the welfare state: Level not higher, distribution not more equitable. *Journal of Comparative Policy Analysis: Research and Practice* 2: 91–125. CrossRef.

WVSA – World Values Survey Association (2014) World values survey 1981-2014 longitudinal aggregate v.20141125. http://www.worldvaluessurvey.org

A Appendix

A.1 Data

We cleaned the IMF and OECD fiscal data to remove unreliable observations. We explain the most important parts of this cleaning here. Full detail can be found in our code which we have placed on the Motu website (www.motu.org.nz).

A.1.1 Modern vs. Historical GFS

The IMF data from 1972 – 1989 is classified using the 'historical' 1986 definitions while the data from 1990 onwards are classified using the 'modern' 2001 format. We followed the IMF's guidelines for reclassifying data from 1986 to 2001 format. The key differences between the historical and modern format is that the historical outlays include gross purchases of capital assets in the relevant COFOG category, while modern only reports net purchases of capital in the functional categories. There is no way to convert 1986 expenditure data exactly to the 2001 definition because there is no information to allocate sales of capital assets to the various functions. There are also issues with how revenues of government enterprises and social contributions for government employees are reported. Finally environmental protection is a new category in GFS2001.

In addition the modern IMF GFS statistics include both accrual and cash based definitions of fiscal variables – with neither versions of the variables offering complete coverage. For this reason we use the cash data where possible, and then for the remainder we use the accrual data – modified to be more comparable to the cash data. The modification process is as follows: first we look at cases where we have both the accrual and cash data. Then we calculate the 10% trimmed mean of the ratio of cash to accrual (separately for each variable). Finally the accrual data is multiplied by this (variable specific) ratio.

The OECD data and IMF fiscal data appear to be compiled differently. To make them comparable we use the same method as we did for converting accrual to cash data.

A.1.2 Dropping of countries with unreliable data

We inspected the fiscal data for all countries in our analysis. Where the data looked unreliable that country was dropped – at least for the period where the data looked unstable. In particular we included most countries where none of their key fiscal variables changed by more than 7 percentage points since last observed (usually the previous year). For countries that had changes larger than 7 percentage points we inspected to see if these changes plausibly reflected real changes rather than just questionable data. For example, our data showed Iceland's unproductive expenditures increased by over 10 percentage points of GDP in 2008, but given their massive banking failure that year, such variation is to be expected, and so Iceland is included in our analysis. On the hand, the 15 percentage point increase in NZ productive expenditure as a share of GDP from 2007 to 2009 is judged to be inaccurate data, and so New Zealand is excluded from our analysis. We limit our focus to high and middle income countries excluding low income countries such as India.

A.2 Tables and Figures

Table A.1: Fiscal variable classifications

Symbol	THEORETICAL CATEGORY	IMF FUNCTIONAL CATEGORY
DT	Distortionary taxation	Taxation on income and profit Social security contributions Taxation on payroll and manpower Taxation on property
NDT	Non-distortionary taxation	Taxes on goods and services
PE	Productive expenditures	General public services Defence Education Health Housing Transport and communication
UE	Unproductive expenditures	Social security and welfare Recreation Economic services
OR	Other revenues	
OE	Other expenditure	
BS	Budget surplus	We define this as the residual: $DT_t + NDT_t + OR_t - PE_t -$ $UE_t - OE_t \equiv BS_t$

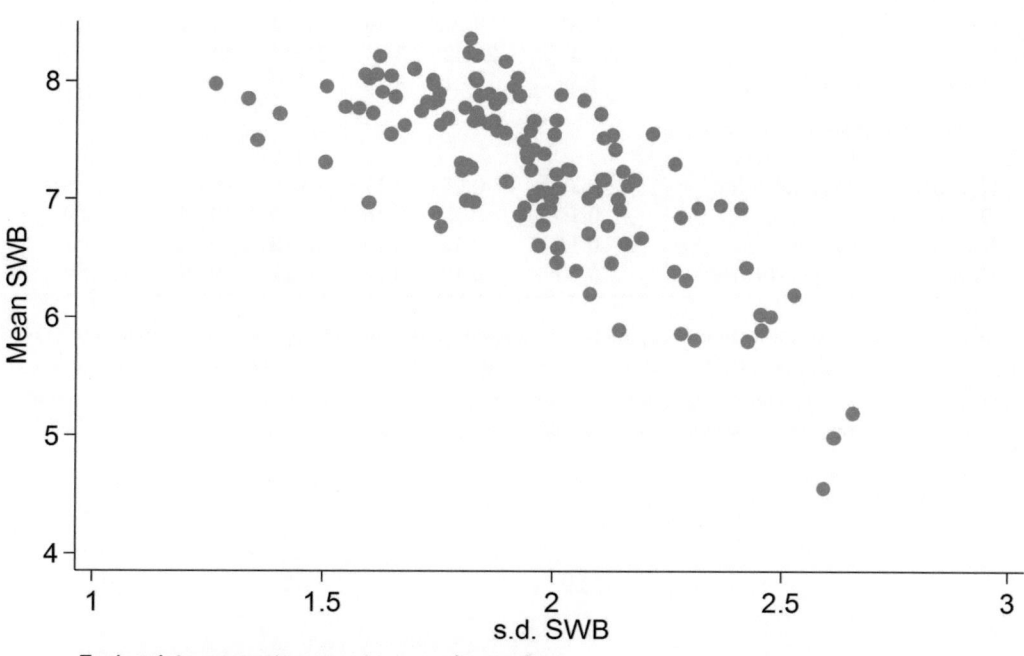

Each point represents a country-year observation.
Only plots country-year observations used in base central government regression.

Figure A.1: Scatter plot of mean SWB vs. s.d. SWB

Table A.2: Country-level variable summary statistics

	Mean	Median	s.d	Min	Max	Number country-year obs
*General Government definitions**						
Distortionary taxation	24.91	24.8	5.92	7.36	37.62	79
Non-distortionary taxation	10.74	11.26	2.73	4.01	15.91	79
Productive expenditures	21.6	22.07	3.58	10.37	29.79	79
Unproductive expenditures	19.39	19.94	4.88	3.09	29.44	79
Other revenues	7.05	6.62	2.79	3.54	18.37	79
Other expenditures	0.12	0.08	0.49	-0.62	3.32	79
*Central Government definition***						
Distortionary taxation	18.46	19.06	6.05	4.3	32.1	129
Non-distortionary taxation	9.58	10.58	3.79	0.61	18.74	129
Productive expenditures	17.14	16.65	4.85	5.05	28.47	129
Unproductive expenditures	17.04	17.38	5.23	3.09	31.16	129
Other revenues	4.63	4.16	2.9	1.36	23.12	129
Other expenditures	-0.12	0	0.95	-6.11	2.01	129
*Macro controls***						
Inflation (% p.a.)	5.87	3.27	9.14	-1.82	83.99	129
Investment	23.48	23.42	3.64	14.64	32.69	128
Unemployment (% p.a.)	7.58	7.1	3.73	1.7	21.4	127
*Proportion of fiscal variable that is subnational government****						
Non-distortionary taxation	0.12	0.05	0.17	-0.05	0.62	69
Distortionary taxation	0.19	0.15	0.16	0	0.54	69
Productive expenditures	0.15	0.13	0.18	-0.18	0.64	69
Unproductive expenditures	0.13	0.13	0.14	-0.31	0.42	69

Notes: The fiscal variables (first two panels) are expressed as a percentage of GDP. Investment is also expressed as a percentage of GDP. All figures rounded to 2 d.p. Figures are based on the country-years that are included in (certain) regressions. * Based on general government sample. ** Based on central government sample. *** Based on proportion government sample.

Table A.3: Individual level variables summary statistics

	mean	median	sd	min	max	N
Subjective wellbeing						
SWB - Central government sample	7.26	8	2.05	1	10	110,659
SWB - General government sample	7.26	8	2.07	1	10	171,804
SWB - Proportion subnational sample	7.33	8	1.98	1	10	93,280
Income scale						
Income - Central government sample	4.83	5	2.43	1	10	65,595
Income - General government sample	5.03	5	2.53	1	10	110,780
Income - Proportion subnational sample	4.87	5	2.39	1	10	51,416
Political scale - 1 = left ;10 = right						
Political scale - Central government sample	5.31	5	2.08	1	10	89,527
Political scale - General government sample	5.38	5	2.06	1	10	137,087
Political scale - Proportion subnational sample	5.27	5	2.03	1	10	74,624
Gender						
Female - Central government sample	0.54	1	0.50	0	1	110,617
Female - General government sample	0.54	1	0.50	0	1	171,696
Female - Proportion subnational sample	0.54	1	0.50	0	1	93,240
EVS vs. WVS						
WVS - Central government sample	0.51	1	0.50	0	1	110,659
WVS - General government sample	0.44	0	0.50	0	1	171,804
WVS - Proportion subnational sample	0.43	0	0.50	0	1	93,280
Age						
Age - Central government sample	46.52	45	17.65	15	108	110,378
Age - General government sample	45.56	44	17.71	14	108	169,876
Age – Proportion subnational sample	46.94	46	17.76	15	108	93,020

Note: Education, and settlement size are also included as controls in our regressions, though (because they are categorical and cumbersome to summarize) they are not included in this table. Age is summarised here as a continuous variable but included in bins in the analysis (see Section 3.2 for details). The N in the last column refers to the number of non-missing observations for that variable, but people with missing values for these personal controls are included in the analysis (with separate missing categories for each variable, again refer to Section 3.2 for more detail).

Table A.4: List of countries included in regressions

Country	Central government regression	General government regression	Subnational proportion regression
Australia	1	1	1
Austria	1	1	1
Belgium	1	1	1
Canada	1	1	1
Denmark	1	1	1
Estonia	1	1	1
Finland	1	1	1
France	1	1	1
Germany	1	1	1
Great Britain	1	1	1
Greece	1	1	1
Hungary	1	1	1
Iceland	1	1	1
Italy	1	1	1
Luxembourg	1	1	1
Malta	1	1	1
Netherlands	1	1	1
Norway	1	1	1
Poland	1	1	1
Portugal	1	1	1
Singapore	1	1	1
Slovenia	1	1	1
Spain	1	1	1
Sweden	1	1	1
Switzerland	1	1	1
Cyprus (T)	1	1	0
Japan	1	1	0
United States	1	1	0
South Africa	0	1	0
Argentina	1	0	0
Chile	1	0	0
Czech Rep.	1	0	0
Ireland	1	0	0
Lithuania	1	0	0
Ukraine	1	0	0

Table A.5: Baseline regressions

Fiscal definition:	Central Government	Central Government	General Government	General Government
Non-distortionary taxes GG			-0.057***	-0.100***
			(0.012)	(0.014)
Distortionary taxes GG			-0.002	-0.005
			(0.007)	(0.007)
Productive exp. GG			0.025***	0.046***
			(0.007)	(0.008)
Unproductive exp.GG			0.016**	0.006
			(0.008)	(0.01)
Other rev. GG			0.039***	0.028**
			(0.01)	(0.011)
Other exp. GG			0.156***	0.159***
			(0.023)	(0.024)
Non-distortionary taxes CG	-0.045***	-0.045***		
	(0.007)	(0.007)		
Distortionary taxes CG	0.005*	-0.002		
	(0.003)	(0.003)		
Productive exp. CG	0.043***	0.048***		
	(0.003)	(0.003)		
Unproductive exp. CG	0.001	0.015***		
	(0.004)	(0.004)		
Other rev. CG	-0.005	-0.010*		
	(0.005)	(0.006)		
Other exp. CG	0.009	0.021**		
	(0.008)	(0.008)		
ln_gdppc	1.041***	1.260***	0.758***	0.635***
	(0.066)	(0.115)	(0.14)	(0.237)
ln_gdppc (t - 3)		-0.405***		-0.026
		(0.091)		(0.24)
inflation		0.002		-0.052***
		(0.001)		(0.007)
investment		0.008**		0.036***
		(0.003)		(0.006)
unemployment		-0.007*		0.007
		(0.003)		(0.006)
N	171,804	169,900	110,659	110,659
No. of countries	34	34	29	29
No. of country-time obs.	129	127	79	79
Personal controls	YES	YES	YES	YES
Survey wave fixed effects	YES	YES	YES	YES
Country fixed effects	YES	YES	YES	YES
R squared	0.122	0.124	0.113	0.114

Notes: Robust standard errors in parentheses. Omitted fiscal category is the budget surplus, and hence the statistical significance reported by the stars refer to statistical difference from the surplus.

Dependent variable is an individual's subjective wellbeing in all regressions. ln_gdppc is the natural log of GDP per capita. ln_gdppc (t - 3) is the natural log of GDP per capita 3 years ago. Personal controls are: age, education, gender, income (as a scale), political orientation, a dummy for survey type, and settlement size (see section 3.2 and Table A.3 for more details on these). Stars denote: * $p<0.10$, ** $p<0.05$, *** $p<0.01$

Table A.6: Subnational government regressions

	(1)	(3)	(3)
Non-distortionary taxes GG	-0.166***	-0.143***	-0.140***
	(0.021)	(0.022)	(0.024)
Distortionary taxes GG	0.023**	0.031***	0.038***
	(0.010)	(0.010)	(0.012)
Productive exp. GG	0.041***	0.021**	0.018
	(0.010)	(0.010)	(0.011)
Unproductive exp.GG	0.005	0.047***	0.037**
	(0.013)	(0.015)	(0.017)
Other rev. GG	0.030*	0.090***	0.082***
	(0.016)	(0.019)	(0.020)
Other exp. GG	0.258**	0.285**	0.291**
	(0.114)	(0.116)	(0.124)
subnational proportion of NDT	-1.148***	-6.275***	-9.737***
	(0.304)	(0.870)	(1.520)
(subnational proportion of NDT)**2		8.768***	4.038
		(1.256)	(7.152)
(subnational proportion of NDT)**3			17.348*
			(9.214)
subnational proportion of DT	0.535	0.695	4.413*
	(0.518)	(1.138)	(2.273)
(subnational proportion of DT)**2		-3.905**	-34.953***
		(1.785)	(8.923)
(subnational proportion of DT)**3			28.685***
			(10.326)
subnational proportion of PE	0.195	-1.040**	-2.362***
	(0.368)	(0.490)	(0.522)
(subnational proportion of PE)**2		0.187	26.730***
		(1.418)	(3.504)
(subnational proportion of PE)**3			-43.822***
			(5.347)
subnational proportion of UE	-0.77	-0.291	5.118***
	(0.487)	(0.551)	(0.953)
(subnational proportion of UE)**2		-4.346**	-5.275***
		(1.766)	(2.041)
(subnational proportion of UE)**3			-50.205***
			(7.628)
N	93,280	93,280	93,280
No. of countries	25	25	25
No. of country-time obs.	69	69	69
Macro controls	YES	YES	YES
Personal controls	YES	YES	YES
Survey wave fixed effects	YES	YES	YES
Country fixed effects	YES	YES	YES
R squared	0.103	0.104	0.105
Adjusted R squared	0.102	0.103	0.104
Akaike information criterion	382,521	382,479	382,400
Bayesian information criterion	383,342	383,338	383,297

See notes to Table A.5.

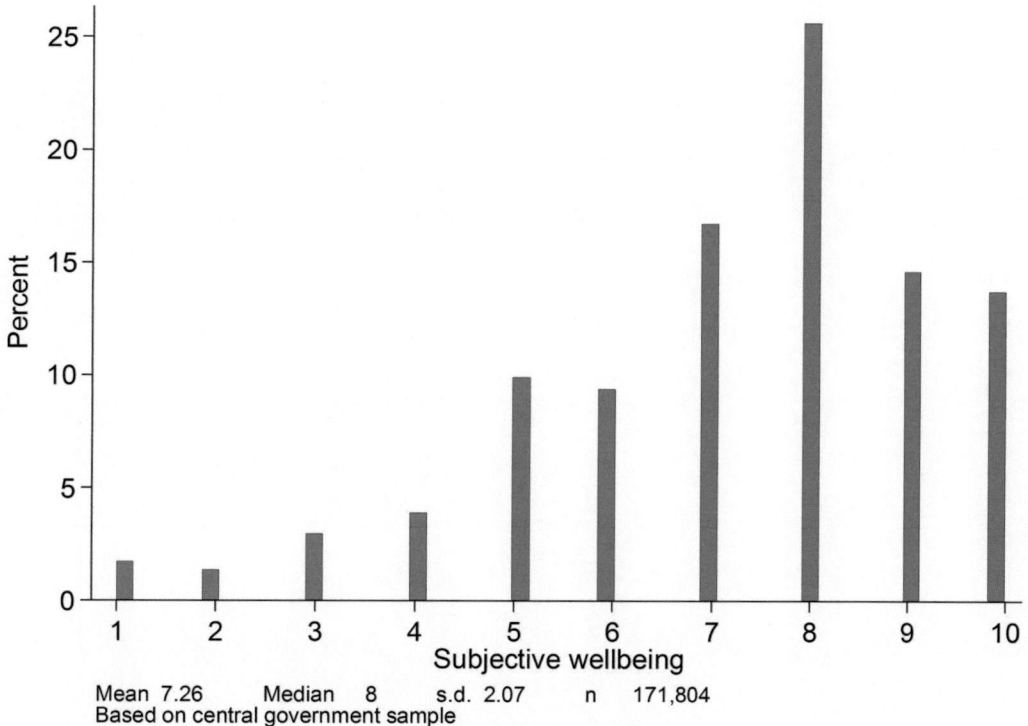

Figure A.2: Histogram of SWB

Volume 3, Number 2, 2016, 1–22
DOI: 10.18335/region.v3i1.123

journal homepage: region.ersa.org

Life satisfaction in Romanian cities on the road from post-communism transition to EU accession

Camilla Lenzi[1] and Giovanni Perucca[2]

[1] Politecnico di Milano, Milano, Italy (email: camilla.lenzi@polimi.it)
[2] Politecnico di Milano, Milano, Italy (email: giovanni.perucca@polimi.it)

Received: 28 January 2016/Accepted: 25 May 2016

Abstract. The literature on life satisfaction in transition countries, and in particular on Romania, demonstrated that life satisfaction significantly differs across rural communities and cities of different sizes. The question addressed in this paper is whether these imbalances are stable over time, or instead, they become manifest in the presence of strong divergences in the economic growth rates of different kinds of communities. Results point out that in the period of sharp economic growth led by large urban areas, as the one experienced by Romania on the road to EU accession, rural/urban disparities in life satisfaction widened, favoring cities of intermediate size.

1 Introduction

The interest towards the determinants of life satisfaction largely increased in the last twenty years. An issue only partially explored by the literature, even if it is gaining momentum in recent years (Morrison 2014, Tomaney 2015, Piper 2015), concerns the relationship between urbanization and life satisfaction. This topic is particularly relevant in the case of transition and developing countries, characterized by huge divergences in the economic growth rates of urban and rural areas.

The relevance of geographic location for individual life satisfaction has been clearly demonstrated and persistent differences across space have been highlighted (Oswald, Wu 2010, Glaeser et al. 2016, Morrison 2011). Some works emphasized lower levels of happiness in cities compared to the countryside (Knight, Gunatilaka 2010, Hayo 2007, Sørensen 2014); others instead report no significant relationship between urbanization and well-being (Appleton, Song 2008, Rehdanz, Maddison 2005, Rodríguez-Pose, Maslauskaite 2012). Moreover, some authors indicate that the level of economic development can affect the relationship between urbanization and life satisfaction, and rural areas are at a disadvantage with respect to urban ones especially in poorer countries (Shucksmith et al. 2009, Easterlin et al. 2011, Berry, Okulicz-Kozaryn 2009, 2011, Requena 2015). These analyses have certainly advanced the understanding of spatial variations in life satisfaction and its determinants. However, a relatively neglected issue refers to the temporal dimension of these spatial unbalances, albeit with some exceptions (Ferrara, Nisticò 2015). In fact, it is not clear whether the disparities in life satisfaction are stable over time or they occur only in the presence of relevant gaps in the economic growth rates of urban and rural settings.

The aim of the present paper is to shed some light on these issues by drawing on fresh empirical evidence from Romania. After the end of the communist regime in 1990,

Romania experienced a period of deep economic crisis, followed by a fast recovery, leading to the access to the EU in 2007. At the regional level, the growth patterns were highly differentiated. Urban areas always performed better than rural ones; from 2004 on, however, these imbalances widened even more. This was particularly true in the case of the capital city, Bucharest, whose rates of GDP growth outperformed all the other Romanian local economies. The evidence presented in the present paper is, therefore, aimed at understanding when these divergences among rural and urban areas of different size emerged and whether and how they mirrored (or not) on the life satisfaction of the resident population. By doing so, we are able to extend previous analyses on the Romanian case (Lenzi, Perucca 2016b) that highlighted important unbalances in life satisfaction across cities and an important penalty for the capital, Bucharest, in line with the original Easterlin's intuition and recent evidence by Piper (2015). In particular, while keeping the urban level of analysis, in this paper we exploit the longitudinal dimension of the large dataset on Romanian life satisfaction evolution and economic growth trends, in the period 1996-2011, that was not sufficiently examined in previous analyses; neither in cross-country studies, e.g. Okulicz-Kozaryn (2012), Rodríguez-Pose, Maslauskaite (2012), Lenzi, Perucca (2016a), nor in country specific studies, e.g., Andrén, Martinsson (2006), Mariana (2012), Lenzi, Perucca (2016b).

The discussion is organized as follows. In the next section, we discuss the literature on life satisfaction in transition countries and we present some evidence on the regional development patterns in Romania between 1995 and 2010. The third section describes the data set and the methodologies used in the analysis. The fourth section presents our findings, while in the final part we discuss conclusions.

2 Life satisfaction and economic growth in Romanian regions

2.1 Life satisfaction in transition countries: a review of the literature

In recent years, a long stream of research focused on the trends and determinants of individual life satisfaction. The main finding of this body of literature concerns the relationship between economic prosperity and self-reported wellbeing.

In one of the first works devoted to this issue, Easterlin (1995) pointed out two main results. The first one, consistent with the expectations of economic theory, is that richer individuals are happier than poor ones. The second, and counterintuitive, finding is that a further increase in income does not have any significant impact on life satisfaction. This conclusion, referred to as "Easterlin paradox" in the subsequent literature, was confirmed in a number of studies on developed countries, like US and Western European economies (Di Tella, MacCulloch 2008). The fall of the Iron Curtain, followed by a deep economic recession and, some years later, by a fast recovery, created ideal conditions to test whether the Easterlin paradox could be extended also to transition economies. Several works indeed addressed this issue.

From the paper by Blanchflower, Freeman (1997), a common finding of this literature indicates that life satisfaction in post-socialist countries was lower, for the whole period of transition and even at the end of it, than the one observed in developed western economies. Given the abovementioned evidence on the association between self-reported happiness and the absolute level of wealth, this result is consistent with the literature on the US and Western Europe (Lelkes 2006).

The relationship between life satisfaction and income growth patterns in transition economies is, on the other hand, less clear. For example, Sanfey, Teksoz (2007) focused on life satisfaction in a sample of transition countries between 1990 and 2002. Their findings pointed out the simultaneous decline of life satisfaction and GDP in the first years of transition, followed by a steady growth of both indicators in the second stage. As a result, in the early 2000's, almost all countries exhibited levels of self-reported happiness and GDP similar to the pre-transition ones. Evidence supporting the consistency of the association between the rise of life satisfaction and economic growth was found also by Guriev, Zhuravskaya (2009) in their study on 28 post-communist countries. Rodríguez-Pose, Maslauskaite (2012) observed that the increase of life satisfaction over time in Eastern Europe was associated to economic growth only for some countries. Romania was among those. This last finding was confirmed also in the country-study by Andrén, Martinsson (2006). Taken together, these results seem to contradict the Easterlin paradox, at least as transition economies are concerned.

Easterlin et al. (2010), however, claimed that for those countries transitioning from socialism to capitalism, happiness and income go together only in the short term (i.e. for a period of no more than 10 years) while in the long period the Easterlin paradox still holds. Evidence supporting this claim was found by Easterlin, Plagnol (2008) in their analysis on life satisfaction in Eastern and Western Germany, and in a study focused on a set of post-communist countries by Easterlin (2009).

Another element that could help explain the common trajectories of happiness and GDP growth in transition economies is the role of urbanization. A broad amount of literature pointed out that the economic recovery of post-communist counties after the first phase of crisis was led by large urban areas and, in particular, capital cities (Kallioras, Petrakos 2010). Therefore, considering the trend of national GDP as a determinant of life satisfaction could be misleading, since it hides the variety of economic paths followed by different regions within the same country. Post-communist countries represent exemplary cases to test whether the association between urbanization and life satisfaction is likely to be particularly closely related in environments characterized by huge territorial disparities in terms of growth and urban expansion. In fact, urbanization is certainly related to positive externalities on individuals' wellbeing, such as better job opportunities, public services and amenities (Puga 2010), but it also generates agglomeration costs like pollution, congestion and social conflicts (Glaeser, Kahn 2010).

Some of the works summarized above incidentally found evidence of territorial imbalances in life satisfaction across settings marked by a different degree of urbanization. Interestingly, all these findings suggest that people living in rural settings are happier than those living in large cities (Rodríguez-Pose, Maslauskaite 2012). Similarly, Hayo (2007) claimed that residents in Bucharest are consistently less happy than those living in any other type of community. Likewise, Andrén, Martinsson (2006) pointed out that, again on the Romanian case, respondents living in the countryside are more likely to be happy than those in urban areas of any size. Finally, Mariana (2012) pointed out that life satisfaction in Romania mainly depends on the availability of resources satisfying the basic human needs.

More recently, Lenzi, Perucca (2016b) conducted a cross-sectional analysis on life satisfaction in Romanian regions, classified according to their level of urbanization, and found that the life satisfaction of residents in urban communities is higher than the happiness of those living in rural areas, with the sole exception of Bucharest. In this latter case, in fact, urban diseconomies prevail over the positive externalities of agglomeration, leading to lower levels of residents' well-being.

On balance, therefore, the literature has not yet achieved a definitive conclusion about the relationship between transition, urbanization and happiness. Moreover, little is known about the evolution of the relationship between life satisfaction and urbanization over time both in cross-country studies (e.g., Okulicz-Kozaryn 2012, Rodríguez-Pose, Maslauskaite 2012, Lenzi, Perucca 2016a) and in country specific studies (e.g., Andrén, Martinsson 2006, Mariana 2012, Lenzi, Perucca 2016b). The conjecture to be tested in the present paper is, then, that territorial differentials in well-being emerged when the development patterns and urbanization processes of different areas started to diverge. In the case of post-communist countries of Central and Eastern Europe, the most intense territorial divergence between urban and rural settings occurred in the second phase of transition and on the road to EU accession. Romania was not an exception in this respect and the next section will provide empirical evidence of economic growth in Romanian urban and rural regions. The focus on the Romanian case is related to two main reasons. First, this country includes several typologies of urban settlements, from very large cities (Bucharest) to second tier cities (e.g. Timisoara, Cluj), from third tier urban areas (e.g. Piatra Neamt, Arad) to rural communities. Second, survey data on residents' life satisfaction are available for a considerably long time span from 1996 to 2011 (Lenzi, Perucca 2016b)[1].

---

[1]More details on the data set are available in Section 3.

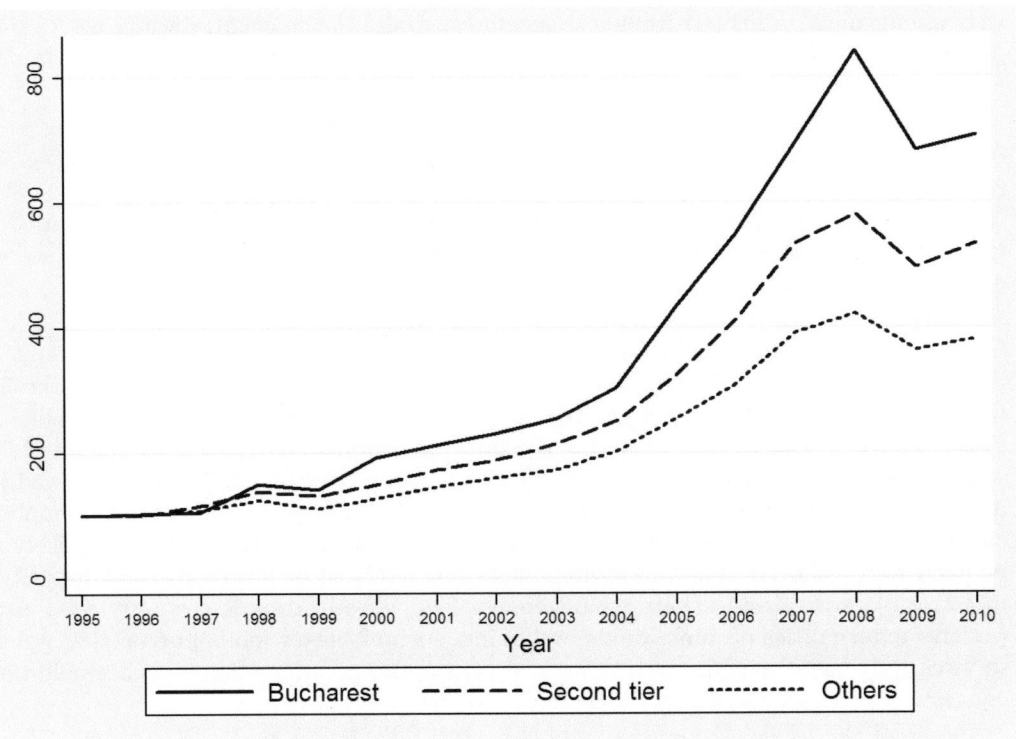

Figure 1: Per capita GDP growth in Romanian regions (1995 = 100)
Source: authors' own elaborations on data from the Romanian Institute of Statistics

2.2 Economic growth in Romanian regions: from the fall of the Iron Curtain to the EU accession

After the fall of the Iron Curtain, Romania experienced, as all the other post-communist countries, a period of strong economic recession. According to the World Bank[2], Romanian per capita GDP in real prices was equal in 1995 to the 85 per cent of its value in 1989. Only in 2003, Romania reached again the pre-transition levels. Within Romania, the growth path was highly differentiated across different typologies of regions.

Figure 1 reports the per capita GDP growth rate of different groups of Romanian NUTS3 regions classified according to the population living in the largest city. Bucharest is a unique case in the national context, with 2.3 (in 1995) million inhabitants living in the urban area. The second category comprehends those regions characterized by the presence of a second tier city, i.e. a city with more than 200,000 residents. Finally, NUTS3 areas including towns with less than 200,000 inhabitants are in the third group.

Figure 1 shows that the first years (1995-1999) were characterized by modest divergences in GDP growth across the three typologies of regions. The gap started to widen from 2000 on, even if, in the short run, it remained relatively moderate. From 2004 on, the year of the accession to the EU of other eight Eastern European countries, the differentials in economic growth for the three groups of regions increased more and more[3]. As a result, the relative weight of urban and rural regions on the overall Romanian economy significantly changed, as shown in Figure 2. In 1995, Bucharest contributed to national GDP for a share of about 15 per cent. Fifteen years later, it accounted for one quarter of the yearly domestic product. In addition, regions dominated by a second tier city experienced a growth of their relative relevance within the country, even if to a lower extent than the capital (from 9.7 to 11.5 per cent). Finally, regions without any large urban areas are marked by a sharp decrease of their share of GDP compared with the

---

[2]Source: http://data.worldbank.org/indicator/NY.GDP.MKTP.KD

[3]The accession Treaty was signed in April 2005, when both Bulgaria and Romania obtained the status of acceding country. The accession of these countries was initially planned for 2004 but Romania and Bulgaria actually joined the EU in 2007. The European Commission officially considers the 2007 enlargement as part of the 2004 one.

rest of the country, falling from 75.4 per cent in 1995 to 63.4 in 2010. The most intense divergences across these three groups of regions occurred between 2004 and 2008, while relative stability characterized the years of economic crisis (2008-2010).

Lenzi, Perucca (2016a,b) provide complementary evidence about the divergence in life satisfaction across cities of different size but without exploring the temporal dimension of these unbalances and their emergence. The analysis of the present paper, then, tries to supplement previous evidence by advancing an interpretation of the spatial and temporal trends of life satisfaction by taking advantage of the concept of urbanization externalities. In fact, as pointed out in the literature on agglomeration economies (Glaeser 2011), the positive economic externalities generated by large cities in the form of job opportunities and higher income are significantly greater than the ones arising in smaller urban areas. Larger and denser cities tend to show greater productivity and wages, as well as to offer wider opportunities for learning and knowledge exchanges, innovation and creativity. Moreover, public services and amenities that may positively influence life satisfaction (see for reviews Rosenthal, Strange 2004, Puga 2010) tend to be supplied in larger quantities in larger cities. On the other hand, increased city size and population density can show characteristics that can reduce life satisfaction. Land rent is higher (Partridge et al. 2009), and, by consequence, the cost of living (Dijkstra et al. 2013) increases. Environmental problems are exacerbated, such as congestion and pollution (Glaeser, Kahn 2008) and unregulated urban expansion (Glaeser, Kahn 2004), as well as social conflict and malaise (Glaeser, Sacerdote 1999)[4]. Yet, as far as positive and negative externalities grow similarly across different types of urban settings, we may expect a substantially neutral effect of city size on life satisfaction. This may the case of in the years characterized by limited disparities in growth patterns across different urban areas (i.e. between 1995 and 2004). Differently, we may expect that the fast and heterogeneous growth of urban areas on the road to EU accession (from 2004 on), possibly driven by unbalanced positive and negative urbanization externalities, widened the gap in life satisfaction of residents in rural and cities of different size. The next sections try to shed some lights on these possible trends.

3   Data and methods

3.1   Data on life satisfaction in Romania

The empirical analysis draws on a dataset pulling together several Eurobarometer survey waves. Since 1973, these surveys have been conducted on behalf of the European Commission with the aim of monitoring public opinion on multiple issues, such as EU citizens' self-reported well-being.

From 1990 Eurobarometer opinion polls were carried out also in the New Member Countries, initially under the label "Central and Eastern Eurobarometer" (1990-1997) and then as part of the "Candidate Countries Eurobarometer Series" (1998-2004). After the first EU enlargement in May 2004 surveys on CEECs were integrated in the "Standard and Special Eurobarometer Series".

However, the questionnaire wording is not always consistent across different studies. In particular, for Romania, availability and comparability of data is limited to the periods 1996-1998 and 2001-2010[5].

The final dataset has been obtained by pooling different cross sectional studies over time and includes over 24,000 records on subjective well-being at the individual level, together with information on some individual characteristics. The literature largely emphasizes the role played by individual factors on life satisfaction (Frey, Stutzer 2000); consequently, the empirical analysis will consider them as discussed in the next section.

---

[4]This point is similarly discussed in Lenzi, Perucca (2016b).

[5]More in details, the survey waves employed in the present paper are the following ones. For the period 1996-1998 data come from the collection "Studies from Eastern Europe – Quality of life diagnosis in Romania", edition 1996 (ZA3645), 1997 (ZA3646) and 1998 (ZA3647). Between 2001 and 2003 data are provided by the surveys from the series "Candidate Countries Eurobarometer Series", edition 2001 (ZA3978), 2002 (ZA4153 and ZA3979) and 2003 (ZA3986 and ZA3983). Finally, for the other years data are available from the "Standard and Special Eurobarometer Series", edition 2004 (ZA4229 and ZA4231), 2005 (ZA4411 and ZA4414), 2006 (ZA4506 and ZA4526), 2007 (Z4530 and ZA4565), 2008 (ZA4744 and ZA4819), 2009 (ZA4971, ZA4972 and ZA4973), 2010 (ZA5234, ZA5235 and ZA5449).

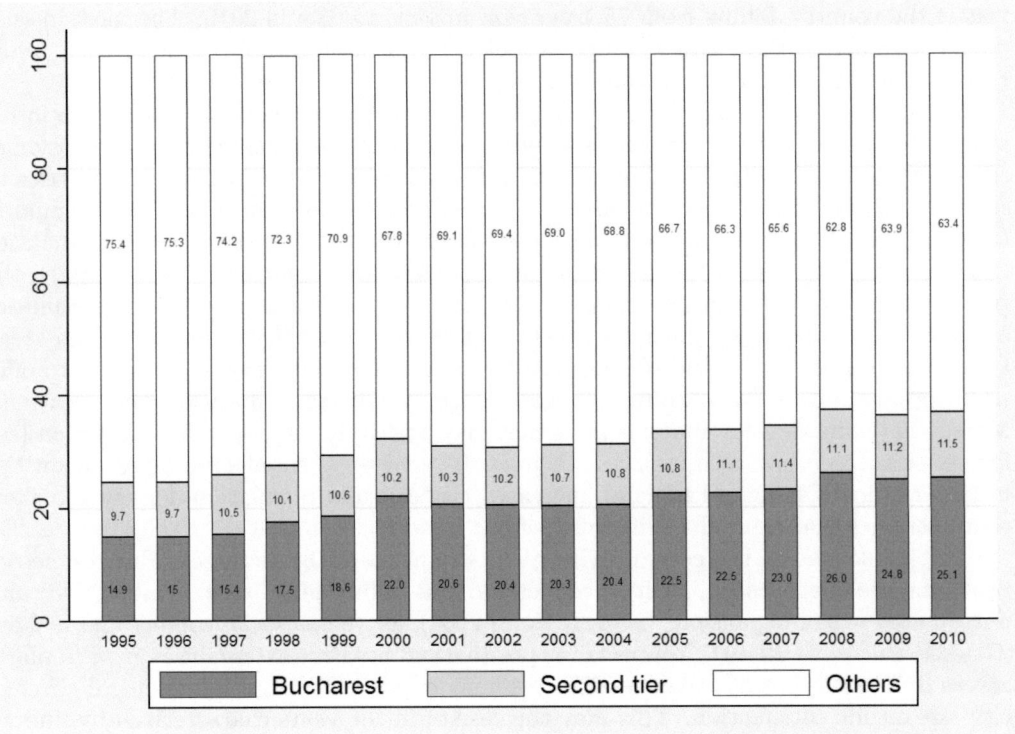

Figure 2: Share of national GDP by different typologies of NUTS3 regions
Source: authors' own elaborations on data retrieved from the Romanian Institute of Statistics

3.2 The empirical model

The empirical model aims at testing the relevance of agglomeration economies on life satisfaction over time while controlling for additional determinants of life satisfaction identified in the literature.

In particular, the effect of city size (i.e. the proxy used for urbanization and agglomeration) on life satisfaction is captured through a set of dummy variables, one for each of the four categories considered. In fact, Eurobarometer surveys ask respondents to indicate the size of the community they live in by choosing from alternative options: less than 100,000 residents (small cities and rural areas), 100,000-200,000 residents (medium cities), more than 200,000 residents (apart from Bucharest, large cities), Bucharest[6]. The answer to this question has been used to capture the possible effects of urbanization generated by the spatial agglomeration of activities and individuals in cities[7].

Besides the dummy variables accounting for city size, the empirical models include several control variables, as suggested by recent reviews on the determinants of life satisfaction (Frey, Stutzer 2000, Dolan et al. 2008, Blanchflower, Oswald 2011). Data availability and comparability across all years considered largely constrained their selection.

At the individual level, the control variables considered are the respondent's age, gender, education, family status, and occupation.[8]. Existing literature indicates some stylized facts about the relationship between individual characteristics and life satisfaction (Dolan et al. 2008, Blanchflower, Oswald 2011). In terms of age, the literature suggests that the relationship between age and happiness is U-shaped (with minimum around

---

[6]It is worth remarking that in Romania there are several large cities (>200,000 inhabitants) but none of them achieves a population greater than 350,000 whereas Bucharest has a population of about 2 million inhabitants (Source: Romanian National Institute of Statistics, Census 2011).

[7]A fuller discussion of the advantages of this categorization is presented in Lenzi, Perucca (2016b).

[8]In the 1996, 1997, 1998 surveys age was coded into 6 categories. For comparability reasons, therefore, we recoded the continuous age variable available in the other Eurobarometer surveys according to this six-point scale. Additional controls at the individual level, such as vote intention, religion, trust, health were excluded because of the limited comparability of the questionnaires over time.

Table 1: Data description

Name	Description	Source	Year
Community size	Size of the city of the respondent (number of inhabitants): Less than 100,000 inhabitants, 100,000-200,000 inhabitants, more than 200,000 inhabitants (apart from Bucharest), Bucharest; reference category: less than 100,000 inhabitants	Eurobarometer	1996-1998; 2001-2010
Gender	Gender of the respondent; reference category: male	Eurobarometer	1996-1998; 2001-2010
Age	Age of the respondent: coded into six categories, under 20, 21-30, 31-40, 41-50, 51-60, over 60; reference category: under 20	Eurobarometer	1996-1998; 2001-2010
Education	Level of education of the respondent according to the ISCED classification. Low education=ISCED 1-2, medium education=ISCED 3-4, high education =ISCED 5-6; reference category: low education	Eurobarometer	1996-1998; 2001-2010
Occupation	Occupation of the respondent: non-working, student, employed, self-employed; reference category: non-working	Eurobarometer	1996-1998; 2001-2010
Marital status	Marital status of the respondent: single, married, divorced, widowed; reference category: single	Eurobarometer	1996-1998; 2001-2010
Per capita GDP	Per capita GDP in the NUTS2 region of residence	Eurostat	1996-1998; 2001-2010

Source: Adapted from Lenzi, Perucca (2016b)

30-50 years, depending on the study); in fact, younger people tend to be happier than adults are but elder people as well are happier than adults are. The effect of age is captured by six dummy variables each accounting for a different age class (under 20 year old (the reference category in all estimations); 21-30 old; 31-40 old; 41-50 old; 51-60 old; over 60 old). In addition, women are generally more satisfied with their lives than men are[9]. The effect of gender is captured through a dummy variable taking value 1 if the respondent is female and 0 if he is male (which is the reference category in all estimations). Moreover, greater educational levels are associated to higher life satisfaction, especially in lower income countries, despite its effect can be influenced by the introduction of other variables as education often reflects also unobservable traits at the individual level such as motivation, intelligence or family background. The effect of education has been captured by three dummy variables each accounting for a different educational attainment level according to the ISCED classification (ISCED 1-2: low education (the reference category in all estimations); ISCED 3-4: medium education; ISCED 5-6: high education). Empirical evidence also suggests that married people are the happiest and divorced the least happy. The effect of marital status has been captured by four dummy variables each accounting for a different status (married, divorced, widowed, single [the reference category in all estimations]). Finally, being employed is found consistently and significantly associated with higher subjective well-being. The effect of occupation has been captured by four dummy variables each accounting for a different occupational status (non-working, employed, self-employed, student [the reference category in all estimations]).

In absence of data on income at the individual level for all waves, per capita GDP in the respondent's NUTS2 region of residence is used as an alternative proxy. The literature, in fact, reports that income is an important determinant of individual happiness (Easterlin 1995). The effect of income is expected to raise self-reported happiness; however, the relationship between income and happiness can be more complex and a quadratic term is introduced to control for possible decreasing returns detected in some studies, as indicated in the literature (Blanchflower, Oswald 2011)[10].

Table 1 provides a summary of the variables described above and their sources.

---

[9]The statistical significance of this effect is less stable and frequently vanishes when other control variables are included.

[10]For example, Rodríguez-Pose, Maslauskaite (2012) report that happiness is more influenced by relative income than by absolute income.

Finally, the empirical analysis includes year dummies. Their relevance is particularly high in the present context. First, these variables can control for the evolution over time of nation-wide phenomena in terms of both social and economic institutional conditions, and of macroeconomic factors at national level, as for instance the inflation rate, assumed to be homogeneous across the country. Second, they can account for the deep socio-economic changes that affected Romania in the period considered, most notably the transition from planned to market economy, the preparation for entry and the final accession into the EU, and, lastly, the impact of the financial and public debt crisis, most of which deeply interacted with the operation of urbanization and agglomeration forces. By the use of time dummies we are able to shed further light on the relationship between urbanization, life satisfaction and economic performance. In particular, following the discussion in Section 2, the early years after accession are expected to be characterized by lower levels of life satisfaction, which is instead expected to grow steadily in the years around accession to the European Union, with some decline in the years of the crisis.

The measurement of the dependent variable is based on the Eurobarometer question asking respondents to indicate their level of life satisfaction among four options: very satisfied, rather satisfied, fairly dissatisfied or very dissatisfied. In this paper, self-reported level of satisfaction has dichotomized; the deriving dummy variable takes a value of 1 if the individual is very or rather satisfied and equal to 0 otherwise.

Therefore, the empirical model to be estimated for any individual i in any NUTS2 r is as follows:

$$P(\text{Life satisfaction} = 1) \quad = \quad F(\text{age}_i, \text{gender}_i, \text{marital status}_i, \text{education}_i, \text{occupation}_i,$$
$$\text{per capita GDP}_r, \text{city size}_i, \text{year dummy}) \qquad (1)$$

This model has been estimated by logit. In principle, the ordinal nature of the dependent variable would require the estimation of an ordered model, such as ordered logit or probit. However, the estimation of a binary logit can be defended on the ground of two main arguments. First, ordered models are based on the assumption that the relationship between different categories of the dependent variable is always the same. This hypothesis has been rejected by means of Brant tests implemented on each single variable (as shown in Appendix A.1). Alternatively, multinomial models could be used. The latter, on the other hand, have a less straightforward interpretation since it would produce, in the present empirical study, a set of coefficients for each regressor and make more complex the identification of the overall impact of urban agglomeration on subjective well-being, which is main issue of the paper. Yet, the main conclusions of the analysis are robust to the estimation of ordered logit models (as shown in Appendix A.1), where the probability of satisfaction is measured on a four-item satisfaction scale. Lastly, in all regressions, errors are clustered at both the year and regional (NUTS2) level.

4   Results

Table 2 shows the estimates of Equation 1 and reports adapted results from Lenzi, Perucca (2016b). Individual characteristics largely show the expected sign and significance consistent with stylized facts in the literature, confirming their relevance as determinants of life satisfaction[11]. Given the high consistency of estimates with existing results, the coefficient of individual variables are not displayed with the exception of regional (NUTS2) GDP per capita, our proxy for individual wealth; its influence on life satisfaction follows an inverted U-shaped form suggesting positive though diminishing returns on life satisfaction[12]. More interestingly, the dummy variables accounting for the population size of the residence area are not significant (Table 2, model 2), with the exception of

---

[11]The full set of individual effects coefficients is available and commented in Appendix A.2.

[12]We are aware that GDP per capita is an indirect proxy for income. Unfortunately, data on income at NUTS2 are available only for a shorter period (i.e. from 2000 onwards). Yet, the simple correlation between GDP per capita and income (computed on those years in which data are available at NUTS2 level) is 0.92 and significant at 1% level. By substituting GDP per capita with income and running regressions on the subsample for which income data are available, findings are qualitatively unchanged. Appendix A.3 reports the results of this robustness check. Therefore, given the high consistency of

Table 2: Life satisfaction and city size

Dependent variable: satisfied/very satisfied = 1	(1)	(2)	(3)
Per capita GDP	0.488***	0.503***	0.477***
	(0.086)	(0.093)	(0.083)
Per capita GDP (square)	-0.022***	-0.023***	-0.021***
	(0.004)	(0.005)	(0.004)
Community size (ref.: less than 100,000 residents)			
100 -200,000 residents		0.106***	0.107***
		(0.036)	(0.034)
>200,000 residents		0.082	
		(0.070)	
>200,000 residents (without Bucharest)			0.130**
			(0.057)
Bucharest			-0.103***
			(0.036)
Year dummies (ref.: 1996)			
1997	-0.196***	-0.197***	-0.195***
	(0.055)	(0.054)	(0.052)
1998	-0.176***	-0.175***	-0.177***
	(0.006)	(0.006)	(0.006)
2001	0.694***	0.693***	0.689***
	(0.074)	(0.076)	(0.073)
2002	0.895***	0.895***	0.892***
	(0.113)	(0.112)	(0.112)
2003	0.607***	0.574***	0.642***
	(0.069)	(0.077)	(0.065)
2004	0.756***	0.760***	0.764***
	(0.091)	(0.091)	(0.089)
2005	0.396***	0.398***	0.396***
	(0.015)	(0.005)	(0.005)
2006	0.378***	0.377***	0.385***
	(0.106)	(0.106)	(0.101)
2007	0.489***	0.486***	0.497***
	(0.087)	(0.087)	(0.077)
2008	0.374***	0.370***	0.383***
	(0.096)	(0.097)	(0.090)
2009	0.396***	0.392***	0.403***
	(0.091)	(0.090)	(0.083)
2010	-0.187***	-0.191***	-0.180***
	(0.059)	(0.059)	(0.048)
Constant	-1.974***	-2.021***	-1.968***
	(0.092)	(0.118)	(0.102)
Individual characteristics	Yes	Yes	Yes
Regional dummies	Yes	Yes	Yes
Observations	24,146	24,146	24,146

Standard errors clustered at the year and NUTS2 level in parentheses *** $p<0.01$, ** $p<0.05$, * $p<0.1$.
Source: elaborations on Lenzi, Perucca (2016b)

those living in intermediate towns with 100-200,000 residents, who are more satisfied than residents of other settlement categories, similarly to findings reported by Rodríguez-Pose, Maslauskaite (2012). This result indicate that people living in large cities are as happy as those living in less populated and rural areas. However, on separating out the effect of the capital city (Bucharest) from that of the other large cities, i.e. cities with more than 200,000 inhabitants (Table 2, model 3), the picture becomes more nuanced. In fact, results indicate that people living in these areas are happier than those residing in less populated areas, suggesting the existence of an urban-rural divide in life satisfaction favoring relatively larger cities (with more than 100,000 residents), consistent with findings by Mariana (2012). On the other hand, living in the capital city is detrimental to life satisfaction, consistent with findings by Piper (2015). With the exception of Bucharest, therefore, Romanian people living in larger cities seem happier than the others are.

Possibly, the unexpected result for Bucharest can be read through the concept of agglomeration economies/diseconomies. In particular, the presence of greater congestion costs, pollution, social conflicts, crime rates, labor crowding, living costs and reduced purchasing power can make the capital city less attractive with respect to other large cities in the country. Above a certain threshold, increased population size seems to provide more disadvantages than advantages and agglomeration costs seem to prevail over agglomeration benefits, as may be the case of Bucharest. Finally, coming to the time dummies, life satisfaction has rapidly grown in the years close to accession; this pattern has been rather stable, with a decline in 2010 at the peak of the European financial and public debt crisis. Nonetheless, even during the crisis, life satisfaction was greater than in late 1990s, when the transition phase was not yet completed, as similarly found by Sanfey, Teksoz (2007).

In order to understand better the impact of transition over time and space, we repeated this set of regressions by splitting the sample in two periods. The first one includes the final phase (1995-2004) of post-communist transition. The second period comprehends the years immediately before and after EU accession (2004-2010).

Interestingly, results for the first period (Table 3) indicate that the role of per capita regional GDP for life satisfaction was negligible and the unfolding of positive agglomeration effects was not yet reached. Rather, urbanization economies have a non-significant or even negative effect (in the case of Bucharest and of cities between 100 and 200,000 residents). This can be related to the fact that, in this phase, Romanian cities were not characterized by huge gaps, in terms of economic growth, compared with the countryside. Consequently, the negative urban externalities like the higher costs of living, congestion and pollution, were not fully counterbalanced by the economic benefits specific of urban areas. Interestingly, Bucharest was also the region characterized by the most intense growth of GDP in the period analyzed. To further prove this point, Table 4 shows the results from an Analysis of variance (ANOVA) on both the average level of satisfaction (measured as ratio between satisfied respondents over unsatisfied ones) and the per capita GDP growth rate by different typologies of NUTS3 regions, i.e. the four groups of communities considered above[13]. Interestingly, GDP per capita growth rate in the period considered does not significantly differ across groups of regions of different size, with the exception of Bucharest. Therefore, the economic growth occurred in the capital city was not associated with higher levels of life satisfaction. Instead, after having controlled for individual characteristics and for the overall level of wealth, the pure effect of city size on life satisfaction becomes negative (Table 3)[14].

---

findings obtained by using the two variables, we opted for the largest temporal coverage and used GDP per capita data.

On a purely theoretical ground, we cannot exclude endogeneity concerns in the form of sorting effects, i.e. satisfied people are more likely to move to happier/wealthier cities. This issue is discussed in depth in the companion paper Lenzi, Perucca (2016b), reporting no substantial evidence of endogeneity and sorting effects, albeit using a different dataset enabling a direct comparison of life satisfaction between natives and migrants. The present dataset, unfortunately, does not allow recording such information in a longitudinal way, even if we are aware that it would add robustness to our findings. In absence of a direct statistical test excluding the presence of endogeneity, however, our estimates are better to be interpreted as robust partial correlation coefficients rather than causally.

[13] NUTS3 regions are classified according to the resident population in their largest city.

[14] Notice that in Table 4 the average level of satisfaction in Bucharest is not significantly lower than in

Table 3: Life satisfaction and city size: 1996-2004

Dependent variable: satisfied/very satisfied = 1	(1)	(2)	(3)
Per capita GDP	-0.137	-0.112	-0.103
	(0.258)	(0.258)	(0.234)
Per capita GDP (square)	0.014	0.013	0.014
	(0.025)	(0.025)	(0.024)
Community size (ref.: less than 10,000 residents)			
100-200,000 residents		-0.100**	-0.099**
		(0.048)	(0.048)
>200,000 residents			-0.028
			(0.075)
>200,000 residents (without Bucharest)		-0.120	
		(0.076)	
Bucharest			-0.236***
			(0.050)
Year dummies (ref.: 1996)			
1997	-0.149***	-0.151***	-0.153***
	(0.032)	(0.041)	(0.046)
1998	-0.214***	-0.212***	-0.213***
	(0.012)	(0.012)	(0.011)
2001	0.542***	0.551***	0.553***
	(0.118)	(0.123)	(0.123)
2002	0.817***	0.820***	0.818***
	(0.118)	(0.122)	(0.122)
2003	0.615***	0.660***	0.693***
	(0.093)	(0.103)	(0.098)
2004	0.931***	0.916***	0.905***
	(0.076)	(0.073)	(0.077)
Constant	-0.532	-0.569	-0.611
	(0.644)	(0.642)	(0.588)
Individual characteristics	Yes	Yes	Yes
Regional dummies	Yes	Yes	Yes
Observations	9,935	9,935	9,935

Standard errors clustered at the year and NUTS2 level in parentheses *** $p<0.01$, ** $p<0.05$, * $p<0.1$
Source: authors' own elaborations

On the other hand, results for the second period (Table 5) describe a very different situation. First, life satisfaction begins responding to economic conditions and incentives. Regional (NUTS2) per capita GDP shows a statistically significant and inverted U-shaped effect on life satisfaction (consistent with the literature and Table 1). Second, cities of more than 100,000 inhabitants seem to offer better opportunities and contexts to achieve greater individual life satisfaction with respect to less populated and rural areas. As commented above, Bucharest represents an exception to this pattern and seems characterized by negative agglomeration effects in both periods. The ANOVA results on the average level of satisfaction between 2004 and 2010 and on the change in GDP occurred in the same period are shown in Table 4. Again, as far as GDP per capita growth is concerned, Bucharest outperforms the other groups of regions. In absence of any individual and wealth control, Bucharest is characterized by a level of life satisfaction higher than the one of regions with less than 100,000 inhabitants (Table 4). However, once taking into account all the individual and regional factors described in Table 1, the net effect of the urbanization economies of the capital city appears to be negative (Table 5). Therefore,

the other regions. Nevertheless, in this case we are not accounting for any of the other controls included in Table 3.

Table 4: Per capita GDP growth rate and life satisfaction by different typologies of NUTS3 regions: ANOVA results

1996-2004				
	Group means		Pairwise comparisons	
Community size	Δ per capita GDP	Satisfied/ unsatisfied respondents	Δ per capita GDP	Satisfied/ unsatisfied respondents
<100,000	1.083	0.386	Not significant	Not significant
100-200,000	1.094	0.368	Not significant	Not significant
>200,000 (w/o Bucharest)	1.167	0.394	Not significant	Not significant
Bucharest	1.582	0.357	+ [all other groups]	Not significant
F	7.70***	2.14*		

2004-2010				
	Group means		Pairwise comparisons	
Community size	Δ per capita GDP	Satisfied/ unsatisfied respondents	Δ per capita GDP	Satisfied/ unsatisfied respondents
<100,000	1.117	0.426	Not significant	-[Bucharest]
100-200,000	1.058	0.532	Not significant	+[<100,000]
>200,000 (w/o Bucharest)	1.169	0.563	Not significant	+[<100,000 and Bucharest]
Bucharest	1.337	0.504	+[<100,000 and 100-200,000]	+[<100,000], -[>200,000 (w/o Bucharest)]
F	4.66***	75.66***		

Source: authors' own elaborations

even if high levels of wealth would lead to a positive payoff in terms of life satisfaction, the purely economic advantages are offset by negative effect on life satisfaction of living in a congested and socially insecure environment.

Finally, we tried to establish a link, if any, between the analysis of the relationship between change in life satisfaction and wealth over time and the main results from the literature on self-reported well-being claiming that economic growth is not associated with significant changes in life satisfaction (Easterlin 1995). In particular, Figure 3 shows the plot of the coefficients of the year dummies reported in Table 3 and Table 5, respectively for the period 1996-2004 and for 2004-2010, associated with the change in per capita GDP that occurred in Romania with respect to the reference years (respectively 1996 and 2004 for the two periods). It is worth noting that between 1996 and 2004 the year dummies and the average growth in per capita GDP follow a very similar pattern, as reported by Sanfey, Teksoz (2007), Guriev, Zhuravskaya (2009), Easterlin et al. (2010). Compared to 1996, the following two years of economic slowdown are associated with a decrease in life satisfaction. The opposite holds for the following years (2001-2004) of economic recovery, even if the differences between the estimated coefficients are, in this case, weakly significant. A different scenario characterizes the second period, between 2004 and 2010. In this case, in fact, the intense economic growth occurred until 2009 is not mirrored by the estimate coefficients of the time dummies. This happens only at the

Table 5: Life satisfaction and city size: 2004-2010

Dependent variable: satisfied/very satisfied = 1	(1)	(2)	(3)
Per capita GDP	0.238***	0.223**	0.278***
	(0.084)	(0.100)	(0.070)
Per capita GDP (square)	-0.015***	-0.016**	-0.014***
	(0.005)	(0.007)	(0.003)
Community size (ref.: less than 100,000 residents)			
100 -200,000 residents		0.186***	0.194***
		(0.067)	(0.069)
>200,000 residents		0.220***	
		(0.068)	
>200,000 residents (without Bucharest)			0.270***
			(0.079)
Bucharest			-0.411*
			(0.229)
Year dummies (ref.: 2004)			
2005	-0.302***	-0.299***	-0.321***
	(0.020)	(0.024)	(0.082)
2006	-0.296***	-0.292***	-0.330***
	(0.056)	(0.055)	(0.060)
2007	-0.124**	-0.113**	-0.174***
	(0.050)	(0.057)	(0.055)
2008	-0.191	-0.173***	-0.260**
	(0.131)	(0.035)	(0.115)
2009	-0.126	-0.103	-0.222***
	(0.080)	(0.089)	(0.051)
2010	-0.761***	-0.745***	-0.838***
	(0.072)	(0.085)	(0.062)
Constant	-0.302***	-0.299***	-0.321***
	(0.020)	(0.024)	(0.082)
Individual characteristics	Yes	Yes	Yes
Regional dummies	Yes	Yes	Yes
Observations	16,223	16,223	16,223

Standard errors clustered at the year and NUTS2 level in parentheses. *** p<0.01, ** p<0.05, * p<0.1
Source: authors' own elaborations

beginning of the economic crisis, in 2010, when the reduction in GDP is also associated to a decrease in life satisfaction. These findings seem to support the Easterlin intuition only under some circumstances. In more detail, during periods of economic recession life satisfaction follows the same path of per capita GDP. In phases of economic expansion, on the other hand, the same evidence does not hold.

5   Conclusions

This paper has explored the evolution of life satisfaction over time and across space in Romania in the period 1996-2010. In so doing, the paper has extended previous analyses on the subject (Lenzi, Perucca 2016b) by underlining that the relationship between transition, life satisfaction and urbanization is far from straightforward and the original Easterlin intuition cannot be translated uniformly in a spatial setting. Moreover, our findings suggest that the temporal dimension plays a relevant role as well. Our results, in fact, seem to support the Easterlin intuition and the hypothesized trade-off between economic growth and individual well-being only under some circumstances. In particular, the analysis highlights that the economic growth benefits deriving from transition have been reaped especially by the largest, capital city at detriment, however, of people's

1996-2004

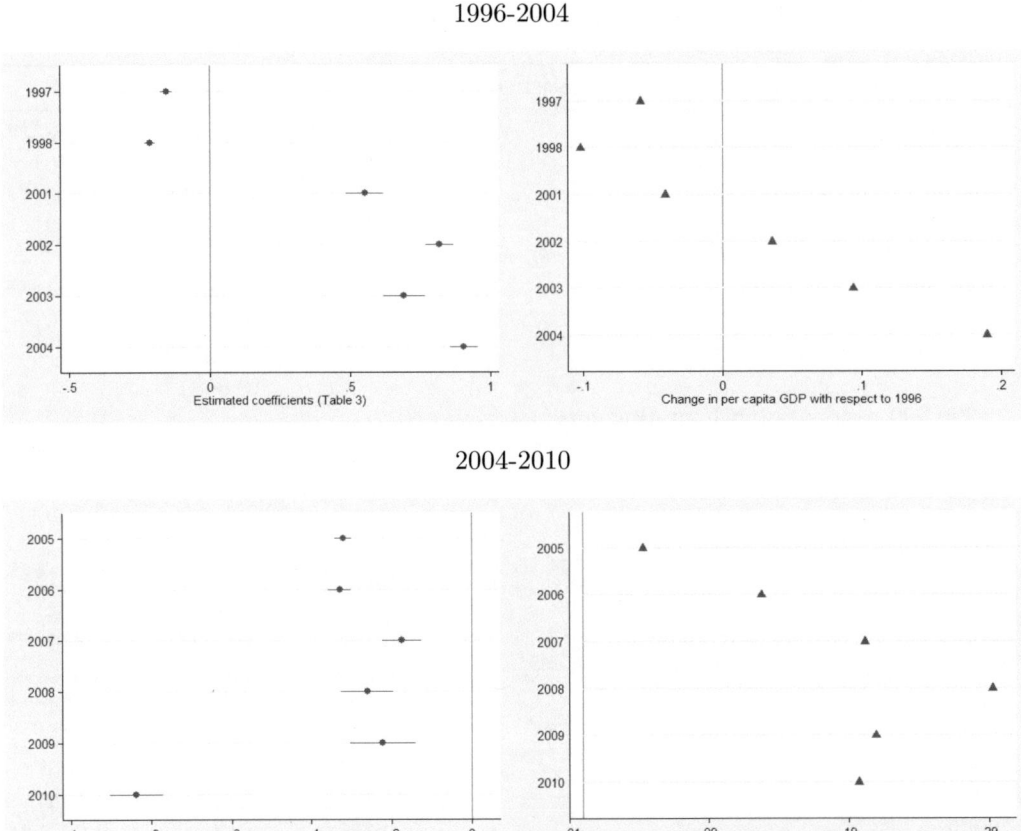

2004-2010

Figure 3: Estimated coefficients and change in per capita GDP over time
Source: authors' own elaborations

well-being. In this case, GDP growth was accompanied by increasing disparities in terms of economic standards with respect to residents of other types of settings, thus translating in the end, into worse well-being prospects. Yet, this conclusion does not apply to medium-large cities. In these cases, instead, economic growth was not characterized by disparities as large as in the case of Bucharest and in the end teamed with increasing life satisfaction. Moreover, in periods of economic recession life satisfaction follows the same path of per capita GDP whilst the same evidence does not hold in periods of economic expansion.

Importantly, our findings seems to suggest that the hypothesized trade-off between economic growth and well-being is not spatially neutral and that under some circumstance there are opportunities to make the two objectives matching. The achievement of such a virtuous combination between growth and well-being (i.e., competitiveness and cohesion, as it could be rephrased in the EU policy jargon) primarily depends on limited (or at least not diverging) wealth and growth gaps. If this is the case, cities and the related agglomeration benefits could actually translate in enhanced individual life satisfaction.

Our analysis certainly presents limitations in terms of geographical extension (and consequent generalization of results) as the analysis covers only one country; nonetheless, these limitations can turn into important opportunities to enlarge the research on this topic. One interesting and promising avenue of investigation concerns a deeper understanding of the interaction between spatial and temporal reach of direct and indirect urbanization effects on the individual well-being of residents of cities of different size across the EU space. We hope to extend our future research in this direction.

References

Andrén D, Martinsson P (2006) What contributes to life satisfaction in transitional Romania? *Review of Development Economics* 10: 59–70. CrossRef.

Appleton S, Song L (2008) Life satisfaction in urban china: Components and determinants. *World Development* 36: 2325–2340. CrossRef.

Berry BJL, Okulicz-Kozaryn A (2009) Dissatisfaction with life cities. *Cities* 29: 117–127. CrossRef.

Berry BJL, Okulicz-Kozaryn A (2011) An urban-rural happiness gradient. *Urban Geography* 32: 871–883

Blanchflower DG, Freeman RB (1997) The attitudinal legacy of communist labor relations. *Industrial & Labor Relations Review* 50: 438–459

Blanchflower DG, Oswald AJ (2011) International happiness: A new view on the measure of performance. *The Academy of Management Perspectives* 25: 6–22. CrossRef.

Di Tella R, MacCulloch R (2008) Gross national happiness as an answer to the Easterlin paradox? *Journal of Development Economics* 86: 22–42. CrossRef.

Dijkstra L, Garcilazo E, McCann P (2013) The economics performance of european city and city-regions: myths and realities. *European Planning Studies* 21: 334–354. CrossRef.

Dolan P, Peasgood T, White M (2008) Do we really know what makes us happy? a review of the economic literature on the factors associated to subjective well-being. *Journal of economic Psychology* 29: 94–122. CrossRef.

Easterlin RA (1995) Will raising the incomes of all increase the happiness of all? *Journal of Economic Behavior and Organization* 27: 35–47. CrossRef.

Easterlin RA (2009) Lost in transition: Life satisfaction on the road to capitalism. *Journal of Economic Behavior & Organization* 71: 130–145

Easterlin RA, Angelescu L, Zweig JS (2011) The impact of modern economic growth on urban-rural differences in subjective well-being. *World Development* 39: 2187–2198. CrossRef.

Easterlin RA, McVey LA, Switek M, Sawangfa O, Zweig JS (2010) The happiness-income paradox revisited. *Proceedings of the National Academy of Sciences* 107: 22463–22468. CrossRef.

Easterlin RA, Plagnol AC (2008) Life satisfaction and economic conditions in East and West Germany pre-and post-unification. *Journal of Economic Behavior & Organization* 68: 433–444

Ferrara AR, Nisticò R (2015) Regional well-being indicators and dispersion from a multidimensional perspective: evidence from Italy. *The Annals of Regional Science* 55: 373–420. CrossRef.

Frey WH, Stutzer A (2000) Happiness, economy and institutions. *The Economic Journal* 110: 918–938. CrossRef.

Glaeser EL (2011) *Triumph of the city: how our greatest invention makes us richer, smarter, greener, healthier, and happier.* The Penguin Press, New York:

Glaeser EL, Gottlieb JD, Ziv O (2016) Unhappy cities. *Journal of Labor Economics* 43: S129–S182. CrossRef.

Glaeser EL, Kahn ME (2004) Sprawl and urban growth. In: JV H, JF T (eds), *Handbook of Regional and Urban Economics*, Volume 4. Elsevier, Amsterdam, 2481–2527. CrossRef.

Glaeser EL, Kahn ME (2008) The greenness of cities: Carbon dioxide emissions and urban development. *Journal of Urban Economics* 67: 404–418. CrossRef.

Glaeser EL, Kahn ME (2010) The greenness of cities: carbon dioxide emissions and urban development. *Journal of urban economics* 67: 404–418. CrossRef.

Glaeser EL, Sacerdote B (1999) Why is there more crime in cities? *Journal of Political Economy* 107: S225–S258. CrossRef.

Guriev S, Zhuravskaya E (2009) (un)happiness in transition. *Journal of Economic Perspectives* 23: 143–68. CrossRef.

Hayo B (2007) Happiness in transition: An empirical study on Eastern Europe. *Economic Systems* 31: 204–221. CrossRef.

Kallioras D, Petrakos G (2010) Industrial growth, economic integration and structural change: evidence from the EU new member-states regions. *The Annals of Regional Science* 45: 667–680

Knight J, Gunatilaka R (2010) The rural–urban divide in China: Income but not happiness? *Journal of Development Studies* 46: 506–534. CrossRef.

Lelkes O (2006) Knowing what is good for you: Empirical analysis of personal preferences and the "objective good". *The Journal of Socio-Economics* 35: 285–307

Lenzi C, Perucca G (2016a) Are urbanized areas source of life satisfaction? Evidence from EU regions. *Papers in Regional Science*. CrossRef.

Lenzi C, Perucca G (2016b) Life satisfaction across cities: evidence from romania. *Journal of Development Studies*. CrossRef.

Mariana CC (2012) Sources of variation in quality of life in Romania. *Procedia-Social and Behavioral Sciences* 58: 645–654. CrossRef.

Morrison PS (2011) Local expressions of subjective well-being: The New Zealand experience. *Regional Studies* 45: 1039–1058. CrossRef.

Morrison PS (2014) The measurement of regional growth and well-being. In: Fischer MM, Nijkamp P (eds), *Handbook of regional growth*. Springer Verlag, Berlin, Heidelberg, 277–289. CrossRef.

Okulicz-Kozaryn A (2012) Income and well-being across European provinces. *Social Indicators Research* 106: 371–392. CrossRef.

Oswald AJ, Wu S (2010) Objective confirmation of subjective measures of human well-being: Evidence from U.S.A. *Science* 327: 576–579. CrossRef.

Partridge, M D andRickman DS, Kamar A, Olfert MR (2009) Do new economic geography agglomeration shadows underlie current population dynamics across the urban hierarchy? *Papers in Regional Science* 88: 445–466. CrossRef.

Piper AT (2015) Europe's capital cities and the happiness penalty: an investigation using the European Social Survey. *Social Indicators Research* 123: 103–126. CrossRef.

Puga D (2010) The magnitude and causes of agglomeration economies. *Journal of Regional Science* 50: 203–219. CrossRef.

Rehdanz K, Maddison D (2005) Climate and happiness. *Ecological Economics* 52: 111–125. CrossRef.

Requena F (2015) Rural-urban living and level of economic development as factors in subjective well-being. *Social Indicators Research*. CrossRef.

Rodríguez-Pose A, Maslauskaite K (2012) Can policy make us happier? individual characteristics, socio-economic factors and life satisfaction in Central and Eastern Europe. *Cambridge Journal of Regions, Economy and Society* 5: 77–96. CrossRef.

Rosenthal SS, Strange WC (2004) Evidence on the nature and sources of agglomeration economies. In: Henderson J, Thisse JF (eds), *Handbook of Urban and Regional Economics*, Volume 4. Elsevier, Amsterdam, 2119–2172. CrossRef.

Sanfey P, Teksoz U (2007) Does transition make you happy? *Economics of Transition* 15: 707–731. CrossRef.

Shucksmith M, Cameron S, Merridew T, Pichler F (2009) Urban-rural differences in quality of life across the European Union. *Regional Studies* 43: 1275–1289. CrossRef.

Sørensen JF (2014) Rural-urban differences in life satisfaction: Evidence from the European Union. *Regional Studies* 48: 1451–1466. CrossRef.

Tomaney J (2015) Region and place iii: well-being. Progress in human geography. CrossRef.

A   Appendix

A.1   Appendix A. Ordered logistic results

Table A.1 reports the results from an ordered logistic regression on the four level of life satisfaction, employing the same specification of model (3), Table 2. The interpretation of the coefficients and their significance are consistent with those discussed in the main paper (see Table 2 and Table A.2). Nevertheless, the Brant test rejected the hypothesis on the validity of the parallel regression assumption (Table A.1) for several variables making the binomial logit model more suitable for the empirical analysis of this paper.

Table A.1: Life satisfaction, individual and regional characteristics: ordered logit results

Dependent variable: level of satisfaction (1-4)	(3)	Brant test (chi2)
Gender: female	-0.036	8.91**
	(0.025)	
Age: 21-30	-0.339***	3.16
	(0.047)	
Age: 31-40	-0.488***	4.37o
	(0.037)	
Age: 41-50	-0.636***	11.25***
	(0.040)	
Age: 51-60	-0.570***	9.25***
	(0.060)	
Age: over 60	-0.472***	5.80*
	(0.077)	
Education: medium level	-0.014	13.56***
	(0.040)	
Education: high level	0.471***	2.72
	(0.064)	
Occupation: employed	0.546***	22.28***
	(0.030)	
Occupation: self employed	0.545***	0.27
	(0.041)	
Occupation: student	0.728***	13.03***
	(0.115)	
Marital status: widowed	-0.329***	0.67
	(0.056)	
Marital status: divorced	-0.421***	0.42
	(0.072)	
Marital status: married	0.096***	4.62*
	(0.037)	
Per capita GDP	0.433***	8.99**
	(0.086)	
Per capita GDP (square)	-0.020***	12.23***
	(0.005)	
Community size (ref.: less than 10,000 residents)		
100 -200,000 residents	0.103*	3.61
	(0.053)	
>200,000 residents (without Bucharest)	0.120*	4.18o
	(0.062)	
Bucharest	-0.027	8.91**
	(0.020)	
Year dummies	Yes	
Regional dummies	Yes	
Constant cut 1	0.006	
	(0.203)	
Constant cut 2	1.902***	
	(0.157)	
Constant cut 3	4.850***	
	(0.178)	
Observations	24,146	

Standard errors clustered at the year and NUTS2 level in parentheses; *** p <0.01, ** <0.05, * p <0.1, o p <0.15
Reference categories: under 21 (age), low level (education), non-working (occupation), single (marital status), less than 100,000 residents (community size).

A.2   Life satisfaction and individual characteristics of the respondents

As discussed in Section 3.2, life satisfaction was regressed on a set of individual characteristics. Results are reported in Table A.2. The three models in Table A.2 differ according to the typology of regional controls included (Table 2). Among other things, our findings indicate that younger people are happier than older people, with a U-shaped effect: people aged between 51-60 are happier than those aged between 41-50, and people aged over 60 are even happier than those aged between 31-40. Highly educated people are also happier with respect to those with low educational attainment. Employed, self-employed and students are more satisfied than people that do not work. Married people are also happier than singles, whereas divorcees and widows/widowers are less satisfied than singles. Finally, females do not appear to be happier than males. These effects are consistent across all models displayed in Tables 3 to 5. It is important to remember that the interpretation of these individual effects has to be done in relative terms with respect to the reference cases (mentioned in the note to Table A.2). As to the age effect, in particular, the coefficient of the dummy variables indicate that the effect of age is U-shaped, with a minimum around 40–50 years. Dolan et al. (2008) as well as Blanchflower, Oswald (2011) report that generally the minimum is between 30 and 50, depending on the study. Moreover, Dolan et al. (2008) indicate that, even if women tend to be happier than men are, the statistical significance of its effect frequently disappears when other controls are inserted.

Table A.2: Life satisfaction and individual characteristics of the respondents

Dependent variable: satisfied/very satisfied = 1	(1)	(2)	(3)
Gender: female	-0.012	-0.014	-0.013
	(0.028)	(0.028)	(0.028)
Age: 21-30	-0.304***	-0.310***	-0.313***
	(0.036)	(0.042)	(0.040)
Age: 31-40	-0.422	-0.426	-0.426
	(.)	(.)	(.)
Age: 41-50	-0.574***	-0.578***	-0.583***
	(0.077)	(0.078)	(0.078)
Age: 51-60	-0.558***	-0.562***	-0.565***
	(0.046)	(0.047)	(0.046)
Age: over 60	-0.373***	-0.375***	-0.377***
	(0.095)	(0.095)	(0.094)
Education: medium level	-0.076	-0.081	-0.076
	(0.050)	(0.051)	(0.050)
Education: high level	0.492***	0.472***	0.477***
	(0.079)	(0.080)	(0.081)
Occupation: employed	0.536***	0.530***	0.523***
	(0.045)	(0.044)	(0.043)
Occupation: self employed	0.540***	0.547***	0.551***
	(0.064)	(0.065)	(0.064)
Occupation: student	0.726***	0.720***	0.709***
	(0.085)	(0.092)	(0.087)
Marital status: widowed	-0.306***	-0.304***	-0.303***
	(0.096)	(0.097)	(0.098)
Marital status: divorced	-0.423***	-0.426***	-0.427***
	(0.064)	(0.066)	(0.066)
Marital status: married	0.101***	0.104***	0.106***
	(0.021)	(0.020)	(0.023)
Constant	-3.184***	-3.296***	-3.049***
	(0.338)	(0.389)	(0.320)
GDP per capita	Yes	Yes	Yes
Community size	No	Yes	Yes
Year dummies	Yes	Yes	Yes
Regional dummies	Yes	Yes	Yes
Observations	24,146	24,146	24,146

Standard errors clustered at the year and NUTS2 level in parentheses; *** p <0.01, ** p <0.05, * p <0.1

Reference categories: under 21 (age), low level (education), non-working (occupation), single (marital status).

A.3   Life satisfaction and the role of regional income per capita

Table A.3: Life satisfaction and the role of regional income per capita

Dependent variable: satisfied/very satisfied = 1	(1)	(2)	(3)
Net disposable income	0.038**	0.034	0.049***
	(0.018)	(0.021)	(0.013)
Net disposable income (square)	-0.000**	-0.000*	-0.000***
	(0.000)	(0.000)	(0.000)
Community size (ref: less than 100,000 residents)			
100 -200,000 residents		0.185***	0.194***
		(0.066)	(0.066)
>200,000 residents		0.185***	
		(0.060)	
>200,000 residents (without Bucharest)			0.265***
			(0.078)
Bucharest			-0.394*
			(0.205)
Constant	-0.863***	-1.505***	-1.432***
	(0.068)	(0.384)	(0.445)
Individual characteristics	Yes	Yes	Yes
Regional dummies	Yes	Yes	Yes
Year dummies	Yes	Yes	Yes
Observations	16,223	16,223	16,223

Standard errors clustered at the year and NUTS2 level in parentheses. *** p <0.01, ** p <0.05, * p <0.1

Volume 3, Number 2, 2016, 103–124
DOI: 10.18335/region.v3i2.130

journal homepage: region.ersa.org

The Journal of ERSA
Powered by WU

Pride in the city*

Philip S. Morrison[1]

[1] Victoria University of Wellington, Wellington, New Zealand (email: philip.morrison@vuw.ac.nz)

Received: 16 March 2016/Accepted: 17 October 2016

Abstract. Urban pride is an individual and collective response to living in a given city. Unlike other emotions such as life satisfaction or happiness with which it is weakly positively correlated, pride involves stake holding; to be proud of something requires having an investment in its success emotionally, financially or culturally.

For this study I specify a multilevel model based on responses to a five category survey question which asks residents how proud they are in the 'look and feel of their city'. Responses to the 2008 survey are distributed over almost 6000 residents across 12 cities in New Zealand. Although the primary variation is among individuals, urban pride also varies by city and I show how differences in urban context affect the way different types of stake holding temper urban pride.

JEL classification: R19, R590, I390, H890

Key words: Pride, urban pride, civic pride, city, social identity, multilevel model, New Zealand, Quality of Life Survey

Pride is an emotion that has profound economic consequences and indeed consequences for all areas of human activity (Boulding 1987, pp. 15–16)

1 Introduction

Almost thirty years ago Kenneth E. Boulding proposed a link between power, planning, and pride in a paper entitled, '*The economics of pride and shame*' (Boulding 1987).

---

*Successive drafts of this paper have been presented over the last four years and I wish to acknowledge the feedback received. An initial presentation was made on 23 August 2012 to the Geography, Environmental and Development Studies Seminar series at Victoria University of Wellington, a year later on 10th October, 2013 to the National Institute of Demographic and Economic Analysis (NIDEA) at the University of Waikato. A later version was presented to the Department of Geography, University of Otago on 2nd October, 2014. The case study was also used as an application of multilevel modelling in a keynote address to the Oceania Stata User Group Meeting in Sydney, on 28 September, 2016 under the title 'Multilevel estimation of contextual effects'.

Several people have commented on earlier drafts. Professor Jacques Poot, University of Waikato, made constructive comments on an earlier manuscript. Dr Michael Thomas, Faculty of Spatial Sciences, University of Groningen, made a number of valuable suggestions on the model, some of which I have adopted and others of which I will address in subsequent work. Dr Tom Collins, School of Geography, University of Leeds whose work on civic pride I drew on in the literature review was kind enough to read the penultimate manuscript and he made several points which I've now included in the paper. I also wish to acknowledge the literature review on this topic initially undertaken by Robert Nairn as part of his honours research essay in 2010. Finally, I wish to thank the three anonymous referees whose comments have strengthened the paper. As usual the responsibility for any errors remain mine.

Economists, he observed, simply assume that preferences are given but in practice our preferences are strongly determined by our identity which depends very much on the community we live in.

This same relationship was recognised by New Zealand's Wellington Regional Council when it wrote,

> *Despite the limitations in being able to monitor our progress regionally, it is known that residents with a strong sense of pride and a sense of community are key to building strong, socially sustainable and connected communities. These people will act as advocates for their region and promote the positive aspects their region has to offer and contribute to improving their neighbourhood* (Wellington Regional Council 2011, p. 35)

Notwithstanding the frequent appearance of the term pride in the urban and regional planning discourse very little attention has been paid to the role of urban pride; how it forms in individuals, how it is distributed among residents within and between cities, and above all how it is used in decision making. This lacunae exists in spite of the increasing attention being paid to the way emotion motivates behaviour in general (Davidson et al. 2007), collectively (Sullivan 2014b, von Scheve, Ismer 2013), and within individuals (Lea, Webley 1997)[1].

At the same time it is important to differentiate pride from a number of other emotions that are receiving attention, such as life satisfaction and happiness. Pride is unique among the emotions in the way it is tied to stake holding for one only feels pride (or shame) in people, events, or places in which one has a stake, through investment, ownership, or membership.

In this paper I ask three questions. To what extent does urban pride reflects the stake people have in their city? What is the relative role of the city and the individual in the measure of pride? And what characteristics of the city influence the way urban pride responds to stake holding? Each of these questions is addressed by analysing responses to a unique question on urban pride asked in the 2008 New Zealand Quality of Life Survey.

The paper makes four contributions to the urban and regional literature. Firstly, it introduces urban pride as a distinct emotion expressed by most respondents in their city. Secondly, the paper identifies and tests for the several types of urban stake holding. Thirdly, it shows how levels of urban pride vary across residents and cities. And fourthly, it explores the way characteristics of the city can modify the impact of stake holding on urban pride.

1.1 Outline

The paper is in eight sections. Section 2 gathers the scattered literature on pride in support of its defining characteristics and draws a working distinction between *civic* pride and *urban* pride. Section 3 introduces the New Zealand Quality of Life Survey. The idea of interacting characteristics of the city with attributes of the individual is integral to the multilevel model introduced in Section 4. The random intercepts model is estimated in Section 5, selected measures of city context are introduced in Section 6, and the multilevel model itself is estimated in Section 7. The paper concludes in Section 8.

2 Pride

Pride is not simply another measure of wellbeing - it is an emotion that results from having a stake in someone, something, or some place. For example: 'I am proud of *my* performance', 'I am proud *we* won gold at the Olympics', or, 'I am proud of *my* city'[2]. The opposite of pride is shame, which also depends on stake holding, as in 'I am ashamed of my performance, my country or my city'.

---

[1]Despite the attention emotions receive in the Davidson et al. (2007) collection, pride as such is not given any attention and this appears to also be the case in papers published so far in the journal Emotion, Space and Society, with the possible exception of Bennett (2013).

[2]As Rosenblatt (1988) points out, one may admire (and envy) a stranger's achievements, but one is not 'proud of' a stranger.

The essential point about pride is that it is based on a prior belief that one has played a role or made a difference in generating the phenomena, event, or condition of interest, even if only in a secondary or peripheral way. Most followers of sports teams feel they contribute simply by being a fan and they are proud of that contribution. Most citizens of countries feel some degree of pride in their country simply because they are born with the right to permanent residence.

Research on pride is scattered over four quite different literatures and each has implications for how we might think about the pride we express in our cities. The psychology literature addresses the way pride regulates individual behaviour (Reissland 1994, Rosenblatt 1988). The social identity literature considers the association between pride and group membership and a growing body of work in economics considers the way pride is associated with departures from rational behaviour. Political scientists focus their attention on the pride we exhibit in our country, on national pride.

In psychology, pride has been characterised as an attitude and an expression of personal self-esteem, and is referred to as a 'social emotion' (Haidt 2003). The feeling of pride is something that we absorb socially from a young age because pride is closely linked with identity formation (Reissland 1994). Beginning with the development of self-concept as a child, we learn how to associate actions with positive self-esteem and we gain a sense of identity in order to interact socially (Tracy, Robins 2004, 2007).

Tajfel, Turner (1979) show that the groups we belong to are an important source of pride and that much of our self-esteem arises from membership of collectives. Building on this literature, Rosenblatt (1988) shows that individuals who form a group share the same ego ideal and thus identify with one another: "The assertion of a group affiliation appears necessary to make some of the status 'rub off'." (Rosenblatt 1988, p. 69). Membership of a collective can also help create a sense of self awareness. As Sullivan points out, "At some level, there is an understanding that the events in question are concerned with 'us' and celebrate 'our' achievements, values, standards or goals, which implicitly or explicitly constructs or imagines an 'other'" (Sullivan 2014b, p. 1–2).

Economists have explored the role of pride as an example of behaviour which departs from the 'rational'. For example, personal pride might inhibit an unemployed person from accepting the dole, or encourage others to work harder for no additional remuneration. Pride is also relevant in understanding conformism in consumer behaviour (Wilcox et al. 2011).

One of the collectives in which pride has long been associated is the nation, the "positive affect that the public feels towards their country" (Smith, Kim 2006, p. 127). National pride involves admiration and stake-holding as well as, "the feeling that one has some kind of share in an achievement or admirable quality" (Evans, Kelley 2002, p. 303). Fabrykant, Magun (2015) go on to make a useful distinction between pride based on objective and normative criteria[3]. National pride has been characterised as imagined kinship through shared acceptance of political institutions and norms (Ha, Jang 2015)[4].

The nation and the city are both spatially bound collectives but they differ over the role of choice. Most people do not have a choice of country, whereas it is rare not to have a choice of city therein. Investing in the city is therefore discretionary in a way it is not with the country[5]. This may be one of the reasons why, "the 'sentiment of urban pride' is becoming more and more popular and widespread as a form of identity that often dominates the national one" (Bell, de Shalit 2011, Pachenkov 2014, p. 368). It is

---

[3]They argue that rational national pride requires some objective grounds to believe in a nation's perfection, and normative national pride is not so strongly related to objective achievements and therefore can be more easily manipulated. The practical implication of this difference stems from the fact that in their search for objectively grounded national pride people would be eager to foster country achievements and their maintenance of normatively imposed pride requires in many cases just reliably protected wishful thinking (Fabrykant, Magun 2015). Elements of this argument may well apply to cities, but a more sophisticated question on urban pride than the one available for this paper would be required to test its applicability.

[4]The degree to which national pride originates from 'civic' versus 'ethnic identity' is still a matter of debate within this literature and the results depend partly on whether individuals are being compared across countries (Reeskens, Wright 2011).

[5]For this very same reason however there is a need to pay closer attention to issues of endogeneity in the study of urban pride compared to national pride.

also one of the reasons for the growing attention being paid to city branding (Sevin 2014, Zenker, Rutter 2014).

2.1   Urban pride

There are three main reasons why scholars have begun to pay attention to urban pride. The first has been to identify 'soft' returns as complements to the financial returns to investment. The focus here is on the degree to which local investments enhance pride in the region or country (think most recently of the Olympics in Rio de Janeiro, or London four years earlier)[6]. A second reason is to better understand ways of fostering urban pride (Trueman et al. 2004), notably through city promotion (Anttiroiko 2015). Both these literatures focus primarily on the aggregate or collective consequences of urban pride rather than the way pride is distributed across city residents themselves.

A third reason has been to understand how pride has been invoked in support of urban redevelopment. Williams (1995), for example, has shown how the term urban pride has been used in the United Kingdom to promote a realignment of urban regeneration policy based on public-private sector partnerships[7]. He argues that so-called City Pride experiments of the early 1990s were only superficially about city pride and were more about procurement and delivery of resources for the development of property[8]. As such, city pride has been used as a smokescreen for a much narrower set of interests, public and private (Randall 1995)[9].

In a more recent paper, Collins (2016) considers the way in which cities promote and defend local identity and autonomy through the evocation of 'civic pride'. The contrast between Collin's perspective and the one I take below invites a distinction between *civic* pride as the term is used by various urban leaders and spokespersons, and what I introduce here as *urban* pride, the pride expressed by individual residents in their city. According to this distinction, civic pride refers to pride packaged from the 'top' by city leaders and urban pride to pride expressed from 'below', by individual residents.

Defined in this way civic pride and urban pride represent different perspectives and are likely to be measured and analysed in different ways. For example, Collins applies a discourse analysis to recent urban documents and local media as a way of examining how civic pride is mobilised and promoted within and beyond the city. By contrast, my paper is concerned with how and why urban pride is expressed by individuals and the relative effect of the city on those relationships. I apply a statistical model in order to understand the implied multilevel variance.

One of the possibilities that emerges from the identification of these two types of pride, civic and urban, is that the view from the 'top', may not be highly correlated with the view from the 'below'. One of the reasons for this disjuncture is statistical: civic pride is a packaged average based largely on anecdote whereas urban pride is a distribution based on a representative sample of city residents. The latter can range from very high levels of urban pride expressed by residents who are passionate about their city through to quite

---

[6]There is also evidence that international sporting success can be captured in higher subjective wellbeing (Pawlowski et al. 2014) even if the effect is short lived (Cummins 2009). The propagation of urban pride via the Sydney Olympics also appears to have been successful because, "Regardless of socio-economic divisions within Sydney, the anticipatory effect of hosting an Olympics united residents in feelings of achievement, civic pride and community" (Waitt 2001). The united Germany's quest for the FIFA world cup is another example (Sullivan 2014b,a) (Sullivan, 2014a, 2014b). The collective pride in that responsibility promoted subjective wellbeing and accelerated the convergence of East Germans' preferences towards those of West Germans (Sussmuth et al. 2010).

[7]The City Pride initiative was announced in November 1993 with Birmingham, London and Manchester being challenged to prepare a 'City Prospectus' in "an attempt to provide a coherent vision involving the cultural assimilation of local 'partners' and 'stakeholders', and competitive resource targeting beyond existing bidding mechanisms" (Williams 1995).

[8]The policy was more directly aimed at collective co-ordination of investment and local service provision with a focus on, "sustainable development, and the need to increase integration between land uses and the activities of the various actors in order to improve the quality of urban life" (Williams 1995).

[9]From Randall's perspective the City Pride movement in the UK in 1990s was, "a property rather than people-led vision of urban development with its implicit, if unsubstantiated, faith in its supposed spin-offs percolating downwards to benefit all social layers ....it is exclusionary, allowing participation only to those who can afford the entry price" (Randall 1995, p. 43).

negative views expressed by those who are actively hostile. As I show below, the actual variance is quite wide, complex, and in need of understanding.

2.2 Hypotheses

The broad hypothesis of this paper is that the level of urban pride returned by city residents is a function of their individual and collective stake in the city. Without stake holding there is no urban pride and I propose four types: emotional, financial, cultural, and civic stakeholding. Although these respective stakes can operate independently they can also be reinforcing such as when the emotional and cultural combine, or the financial and civic join forces.

The first form of stake holding is the '*emotional*', the way people *feel* about the city and what it means to them personally. This form of sentimental attachment takes time to develop and deepen and for this reason it is positively associated with the duration of residence. Those residents whose families have grown up in the city and whose friends continue to live there have a major stake in their continuing presence in the city. The 2011 earthquake in Christchurch, New Zealand was a salient reminder of the emotional cost to residents who experienced their city being removed from under them.

The second form of stake holding is '*financial*'. Prime candidates are home owners and those in full-time employment who have the means to invest locally. Their livelihood is tied materially to the fortunes of the city. By extension, those who find it difficult to get an economic foothold in the city are likely to have a lower stake which is expected to be reflected in lower levels of urban pride.

The third type of stake holding I term '*cultural*' and involves those whose sense of collective (as opposed to personal) identity is linked to the way the city meets their cultural needs. Their initial support is tied to the sharing of their location with others like them and their pride in their city largely reflects what living in the city means to them in identity terms.

The fourth type of stake holding I refer to as '*civic*' for it refers to the level of engagement people have with the leadership, administration, and general running of the city.

There have been very few attempts to actually measure and quantify urban pride. Some initial steps were made in response to a perceived reduction in community belonging associated with the restructuring of cities and towns in the United Kingdom (e.g. Wood 2006)[10]. The restructuring of the New Zealand economy in the 1980s and 1990s prompted a similar response when local governments realised that evidence on quality of local life and wellbeing was needed if they were to make credible cases for devolution. The result was the introduction of an on-going survey aimed at capturing the quality of urban life in the late 1990s, the New Zealand Quality of Life Survey[11].

---

[10] Few surveys have asked about pride of any kind. An exception is the World Value Survey (WVS), which includes a question about the 'degree of pride in your work' and 'pride in your nationality'. The International Social Survey Programme (ISSP) National Identity modules come close. They ask 'How close – how emotionally attached – do you feel to ... your town or city' (Kelly 1998). However such a question does not capture pride as a distinct emotion. Both surveys are also administered in New Zealand and the responses have been explored by the author (but not reported here) and offer support for the conclusions drawn on the basis of the New Zealand Quality of Life Survey. The closest the New Zealand General Social Survey comes is a question on satisfaction with services.

[11] Details of the New Zealand Quality of Life Project may be found in http://www.qualityoflifeproject.govt.nz/. In addition to being followed by descriptive reports after each round, the Quality of Life Survey has also been used as the evidence base for several research publications. The first used the 2004 sample to study inter-city variations in subjective wellbeing (Morrison 2007), and was later extended to include measures of accessibility using the 2006 survey (Morrison 2011). In a later study, local economists merged the 2006 and 2008 Quality of Life Surveys in order to assess the role of home ownership on social capital (Roskruge et al. 2013). These last three papers did not formally recognise the theoretical and methodological implications of the fact that sampled individuals were grouped within cities (or by neighbourhoods within cities) and hence that the micro-economic behaviour and attitudes of individuals might vary depending on the particular geographic context in which they lived. The first to attempt to measure context effects using the Quality of Life survey were local psychologists interested in how people's 'sense of community' varied across individuals and neighbourhoods (Sengupta et al. 2013). The focus of their study however was the neighbourhood, not the city.

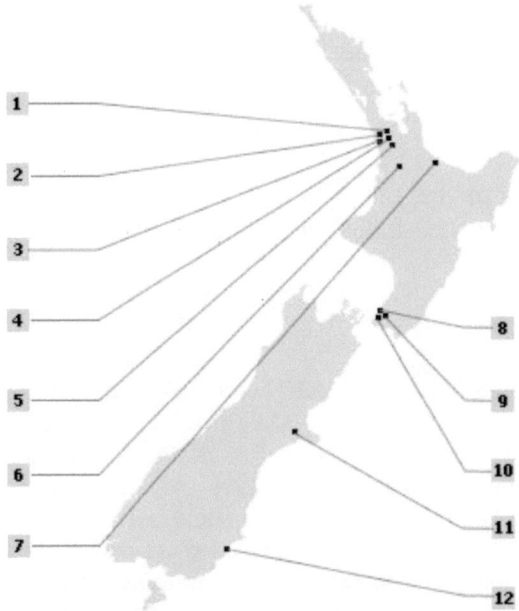

1. Rodney 2. North Shore 3. Waitakere 4. Auckland 5. Manukau 6. Hamilton
7. Tauranga 8. Porirua 9. Hutt 10. Wellington 11. Christchurch 12. Dunedin
Note: Although Rodney is a district rather than a city, I retain the survey's own
description of it as a city.
Source: Quality of Life Team (2009)

Figure 1: The location of the twelve cities included in the Quality of Life project. New
Zealand, 2008

3 The Quality of Life Survey

The Quality of Life Survey is a multi-agency research project designed to explore quality
of life issues every two years in a selection of New Zealand cities[12]. The 2008 survey
was a partnership between twelve New Zealand City Councils and the Ministry of Social
Development. The survey captures New Zealand residents' perceptions of their quality of
life, health and wellbeing, crime and safety, community, culture and social networks, city
council decision making processes, environment, public transport, lifestyle, and work and
study[13].

The 2008 survey was not the latest available at the time of writing. It was selected for
this particular study because a subsequent amalgamation of the four previously separate
Auckland cities to form a new unitary authority reduced the number of urban areas from
12 to 8 thus reducing the range of cities which could be included[14]. The locations of the
twelve cities covered in the 2008 survey are shown in Figure 1.

The twelve cities include almost 59 percent of the country's total population. The
largest city, as of the 2006 census, was Auckland City (404.6 thousand), followed by
Christchurch (348.4), Manukau (329), and North Shore (205.6). The smallest was Porirua
City (48.5). As Figure 1 shows, eight of the twelve cities were located in either the
Auckland or Wellington Metropolitan areas.

---

[12]This account draws on Quality of Life Team (2009, p. 4).

[13]A probabilistic sample of the population of approximately 500 aged 15 years or older was drawn
from each city. The 2008 survey involved Computer Assisted Telephone Interviews (CATI) conducted
with n=8,155 (including 1,500 residents from outside the twelve cities who were aged 15 years and older).
Quotas were set for ethnicity, age, location and gender. Respondents were selected randomly from the
Electoral Roll and a pre-notification letter was sent to potential respondents, who were contacted by
phone for the interviewing. Fieldwork was conducted between 16 July and 28 October 2008. The average
duration of the interviews was 20.3 minutes and the final response rate was 37 percent.

[14]Auckland Council became a unitary authority in November, 2010 when the Auckland regional council
area and seven territorial authority areas amalgamated Rodney district, North Shore city, Waitakere city,
Auckland city, Manukau city, Papakura district, and Franklin district.

Table 1: Responses to the statement "I feel a sense of pride in the way [my city] looks and feels". Twelve New Zealand cities, 2008

Response	Frequency	Percent	Cumulative Percent
Strongly disagree	98	1.5	1.5
Disagree	443	6.6	8.0
Neutral	1,786	26.5	34.6
Agree	3,068	45.6	80.1
Strongly agree	1,341	19.9	100
Total	**6,736**	**100.0**	

Source: Quality of Life Survey, 2008.
Note: Excludes 21 respondents who did not know.

Each city is divided into electoral wards which are a contiguous areal groupings of relatively similar neighbourhoods. The four large cities in Auckland are divided into three to six wards each, Wellington City into five wards and Christchurch into seven. The total number of wards over the 12 cities is 59[15]. The average number of sampled individuals per ward is 103 although they range in size from a minimum sample of 2 to a maximum of 230 people. Some individuals were not able to be assigned to wards thus reducing the usable sample size when wards are analysed from 6117 to 6093[16].

3.1 Measuring urban pride

The measure of urban pride used in this paper are the responses to the following question: "On a scale of one to five where one is strongly disagree and five is strongly agree, rate your agreement with the statement, '*I feel a sense of pride in the way [my city] looks and feels*'."[17]

The general tendency was for New Zealand city dwellers to return at least some level of pride in their city. The responses tabulated in Table 1 show that almost 63 percent (45.2 + 19.9) felt positively about 'how their city looked and felt'. Over one quarter were ambivalent in that they neither agreed nor disagreed, and fewer than 10 percent (7.7) did *not* feel a sense of urban pride as defined.

The urban pride question generates responses on an ordinal scale. While methods of analysing such responses are well developed (Hosmer, Lemeshow 2000, McKelvey, Zovoina 1975) it is now common for quantitative analysis of related wellbeing questions to assume a cardinal level of measurement (Ferrer-i Carbonell, Frijters 2004). The estimated coefficients are much easier to interpret and accord very closely with the relative magnitudes estimated by the ordinal logit model (Kristoffersen 2010)[18].

---

[15]Boundary maps of the electoral wards laid over standard Google street maps may be found in: https://koordinates.com/layer/2159-nz-electoral-wards-2011-yearly-pattern/

[16]Since multilevel analysis involves two or more levels, questions are often asked about optimal sample sizes. Hox (2002) mentions Kreft's 30/30 rule, which suggests 30 groups with at least 30 individuals in each. This could be sufficient for the estimation of the regression coefficients but inadequate for other purposes. If it is cross-level interactions that are of interest, Hox recommends the 50/20 rule: 50 groups with 20 or more in each group. If there is strong interest in the random part, the advice is 100 groups with a minimum of ten in each: http://essedunet.nsd.uib.no/cms/topics/multilevel/ch3/5.html. A slightly different take is offered by Rabe-Hesketh, Skrondal (2008, p. 62): "It is often said that the random-effects approach should only be used if there is a sufficient number of clusters in the sample, typically more than 10 or 20. However, if a random-effects approach is used merely to make appropriate inferences regarding β, a smaller number of clusters may suffice. Regarding cluster sizes, these should be large in the fixed-effects approach if the α_j are of interest. However, in random-effects models, it is only required that there are a good number of clusters of size 2 or more. It does not matter if there are also 'clusters' of size 1".

[17]Administration of four validity tests – content, retest, criterion and construct validity – confirmed that the pride question was sufficiently robust to be modelled. The urban pride question produced similar distributions when it was asked in in 2004, 2006, 2010 and again in 2012.

[18]Decisions to report the OLS results from Likert scales are now routine (see for example Helliwell, Putnam 2004, p. 1438).

Treating urban pride as a continuous measure yields a mean 3.71 on the 1-5 scale (SD=0.87). The highest average level of pride, 4.12, was reported by residents of Wellington City (the country's capital), and the lowest were returned by residents in the City of Manukau, 3.33, located within the wider Auckland region. The intermediate levels of urban pride in descending order were the cities of North Shore 3.90, Dunedin 3.87, Tauranga, and Hamilton, 3.83 Christchurch 3.82, Waitakere, 3.62 Lower Hutt, 3.61 Porirua, 3.57 Rodney, 3.56 and Auckland, 3.48.

In summary, the New Zealand Quality of Life survey has provided the research community with an opportunity to explore the distribution of urban pride across the country's cities. Urban pride is captured in a single measure which asks respondents to declare how strongly they agree they feel a sense of pride in the way their city looks and feels. Following common practice in studies of subjective wellbeing, I treat the ordinal responses as cardinal and will now model this variation as a function of individual stake holding and city characteristics[19].

4 The two level model

Most studies of emotional response apply the conventional OLS 'total' regression model to the relationship between the outcome y and arguments X in order to estimate the *fixed* parameters α and β, where i refers to the individual[20].

$$\boldsymbol{y}_i = \alpha_0 + \beta X_i + \boldsymbol{\epsilon}_i \tag{1}$$

In such a model the random or allowed-to-vary element is captured by $\boldsymbol{\epsilon}$, the mean or expected value of which is assumed to be zero. An accompanying assumption is that there is constant variability in $\boldsymbol{\epsilon}_i$ and no autocorrelation. The assumption is necessary if the variance of the error term is to be characterised by a single parameter σ_ϵ^2.[21]

The application of equation (1) would fail to address two integral features of urban pride: that pride is likely to be contagious *within* the city, as well as being responsive to differences *between* cities. The presence of contagion and inter-city differences violates the i.i.d assumptions of the OLS regression model implicit in $\boldsymbol{\epsilon}$ and renders the occurrence of type 1 errors more likely (Kreft, du Leeuw 2006, Rabe-Hesketh, Skrondal 2008).

A more suitable model would allow average levels of urban pride to vary across cities so that the average level of urban pride in the jth city is the sum of the city-wide average, α_0, plus a varying difference $\boldsymbol{u}_j$.[22] The fixed intercept, α_0, would represent the average level of urban pride across all the cities and the variance, σ_μ^2, would measure the inter-city variability about the average[23].

$$a_{0j} = \alpha_0 + \boldsymbol{u}_j \tag{2}$$

Combining the micro equation of (1) and the macro equation of (2) produces the two-level mixed model of equation (3).[24]

$$\boldsymbol{y}_{ij} = \alpha_0 + \beta x_{ij} + (\boldsymbol{u}_j + \boldsymbol{\epsilon}_{ij}) \tag{3}$$

An initial step in applying this random intercepts model is to estimate the proportion of the variance attributable to differences among individuals at one level and cities at the other. In this null model,

---

[19]Multilevel models are used to estimate context effects – in this case the marginal and cross-level effect of the city (context) on urban pride. Two useful introductions to the method are Luke's study of voting behaviour in the USA (Luke 2004) and Jones et al. (1992) for the UK.

[20]I follow Kreft, du Leeuw (2006, p. 22) in writing random variables in bold, $\boldsymbol{y}_i$ and $\boldsymbol{\epsilon}_i$.

[21]The following account draws on two particularly clear introductions to multilevel models in two fields, geography and public health (Jones 1991, Subramanian et al. 2003).

[22]Although I introduce a layer between the individual and city, the ward variation turns out to simply be a composition effect. Therefore the three level model will not be continued into the multilevel model and j will continue to refer to the city level.

[23]If this equation was used to estimate the relationship between urban pride and the level of stake holding the effect of the city itself would be subsumed within the error term $\boldsymbol{\epsilon}_i$ and go unrecognised as such. By contrast, the random intercepts model (equation 3) allows this inter-city heterogeneity to be recognised.

[24]There is of course also an implicit variable here multiplied by α_0, x_0 which is a vector of ones

Table 2: Intra-class correlation coefficients: cities, wards, cities and wards. New Zealand 2008

Levels	ICC	SE	95% confidence interval	
Cities	0.06	0.02	0.03	0.12
Wards	0.07	0.01	0.05	0.11
Cities/Wards	0.06	0.02	0.02	0.12
Wards/Cities	0.07	0.02	0.03	0.13

Source: Quality of Life Survey, 2008.

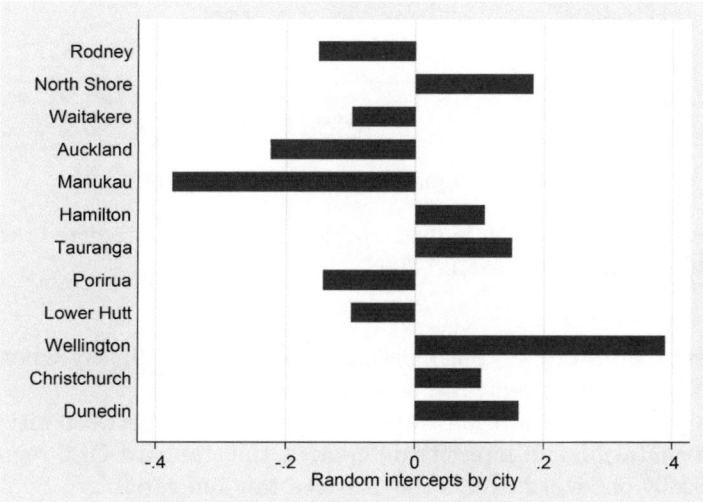

Source: Quality of Life Survey, 2008.

Figure 2: Inter-city variation in urban pride: predicted random intercepts by city. New Zealand 2008.

$$\boldsymbol{y}_{ij} = \alpha_0 + (\boldsymbol{u}_j + \boldsymbol{\epsilon}_{ij}) \tag{4}$$

where the proportion of the variance attributable to individuals is

$$\frac{\sigma_\epsilon^2}{\sigma_\epsilon^2 + \sigma_\mu^2}$$

and the variation across cities is

$$\frac{\sigma_\mu^2}{\sigma_\epsilon^2 + \sigma_\mu^2}$$

which is referred to as the *intra-class correlation* (ICC).

In this application, the intra-class correlation is a measure of the degree to which individuals share the experiences of living in the same city. If the correlation is greater than zero then there is a case for applying a random coefficients model and its extension as a multilevel model. The presumption in such a step is that the differences we see in the level of urban pride from one city to another is not due simply to differences in the levels of stake holding by individual residents (the *composition* effect) but arise in part from differences among the cities themselves (the *context* effect).

An intra-class correlation coefficient of 5.7 percent implies that differences in levels of urban pride across the 12 cities account for nearly 6 percent of the variance in urban pride (Table 2). The rest, 94 percent, is due to the differences among individuals. A similar partitioning of the variance applies if clustering is confined to the 59 wards, however since

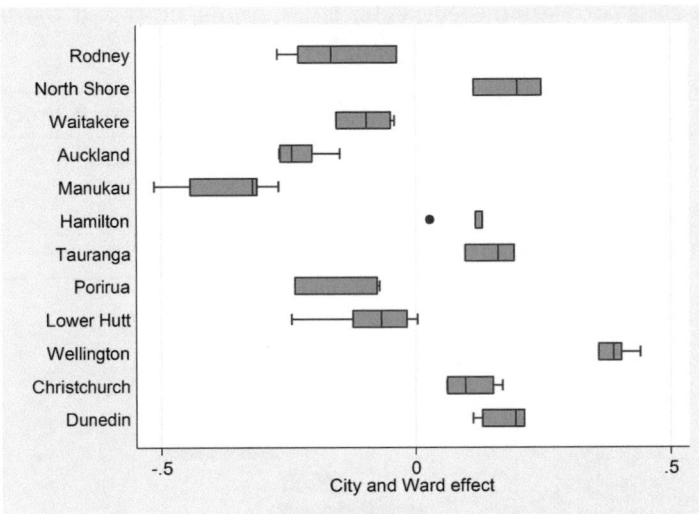

Source: Quality of Life Survey, 2008.

Figure 3: Ward to ward variation in urban pride within cities: predicted random intercepts by wards within cities. New Zealand 2008.

wards are nested within cities, both variances are reduced slightly when they are both included; to 5.5 and 6.6 percent, respectively[25].

In summary, since urban pride varies both within and between cities as a possible result of both contagion and intercity differences, the standard OLS regression model is better replaced by one which treats the city as a random variable.

5 A random intercepts model

The random intercept model of equation (4) implies a different intercept term for each city, $\alpha + \mu_j$; $j = 1, \ldots, 12$. These terms are not estimated directly but we can use linear unbiased predictions (BLUPS) of their random effects as shown in Figure 2. At one extreme, the City of Manukau has a prediction one half a standard deviation lower than the grand mean, and Wellington City almost half a standard deviation higher. These differences in the average level of urban pride across the twelve New Zealand cities are immediately recognised by New Zealand audiences (often with a smile).

Recognising that average levels of urban pride vary across New Zealand cities does not in itself address the fact that urban pride may vary within cities. We can identify variation both within and between cities by adding the neighbourhood intercept term $\boldsymbol{u}_*$ to equation (3), that is, $\boldsymbol{u}_j + \boldsymbol{u}_* + \boldsymbol{\epsilon}_{ij}$. Ward random effects are not calculated directly either but we can overlay their best linear unbiased predictions as in Figure 3. The median in each box reflects the city random intercepts while the length of the boxes (and the outliers) indicates the degree of inter-ward variation within each city.

As Figure 3 shows, the inter-ward variation in urban pride varies noticeably from one city to another, being relatively wide in Rodney and Manukau and Porirua and comparatively narrow in Wellington and Auckland.

5.1 Differences among residents

As expected, urban pride varies across cities. It also appears that levels of urban pride vary by ward. We now turn to the third possible source of variation – differences among individuals themselves.

Nine separate sources of individual stake holding along with two controls are listed under the four headings in Table 3 together with their respective means and standard

---

[25]Similar magnitudes are obtained when pride is represented as a binary variable, i.e. when 1 is set to either Strongly Agreeing with the pride statement or Agreeing and Strongly Agreeing.

Table 3: Measures of stake holding and controls used in the modelling of urban pride. New Zealand, 2008

Variable	Description	Mean	Std Dev
Controls			
Female	Female	0.53	0.50
Health	Health good or very good	0.61	0.49
Emotional stakes			
Duration	Resident in city 10 years +	0.70	0.46
Community	Sense of community	0.55	0.50
Financial stakes			
Owner	Home owner	0.62	0.49
Not employed	Not employed	0.26	0.44
Enough	Income meets everyday needs	0.87	0.34
Cultural stake			
Minority	Non-European	0.23	0.42
Civic stakes			
Safe	Feel safe in central city	0.63	0.48
Clean	No rubbish noticed	0.49	0.50
Council	Councidence in Council decisions	0.46	0.50

Source: Quality of Life Survey, 2008.
Note: The relevant survey questions are listed in the Appendix.

deviation. Each is a binary variable coded so that the expected sign is positively correlated with urban pride. The emotional stake in the city is represented by two variables. The first is duration of residence and we learn that over 70 percent of residents had lived in their city for a decade or more. Notwithstanding this long average association with the city, only 55.3 percent felt their neighbourhood offered them a sense of community.

Three measures are designed to capture residents' financial stake in the city: home-ownership (62 percent)[26], employment (over three quarters) and nearly 87 percent said they had enough money to live on[27]. Having a cultural stake in the city is represented by a single variable, membership of a minority ethnic group, collected here under the term non-European (23 percent)[28]. Three measures were used to identify civic stake holding: whether the respondent felt safe or very safe in their city centre during the day (63.4%), whether they identified litter and rubbish lying on the street (49.3%), and whether they agreed that 'the council makes decisions that are in the best interests of their city' (45.5 %)[29]. The two controls in Table 3 reveal a slight majority of women in the sample (52.8%), and a population where nearly 61 percent of respondents are in Good or Very Good Health.

---

[26]The exact definition of home ownership affects the strength of the relationship between ownership and pride, the tighter or more literal definition the stronger the link. See the Appendix for the definitions used.

[27]This subjective measure of economic prosperity has been selected for two reasons. Firstly, although income (at both the individual and household level) is collected by the survey, the response rates are unacceptably low. Secondly, when people report their perceived ability to cope financially they implicitly consider the local costs of living and these vary from one city to another.

[28]The term European is ambiguous in the New Zealand context for various reasons including the widespread presence of dual ethnicity. In this survey around seven percent of respondents reported dual ethnicity (mainly Maori and European). They have been included here as European as have those identifying as 'Kiwi' or New Zealander.

[29]The base population implied by Table 3 (where all the arguments take zero values) identifies European men in relatively poorer health who have lived in the city for less than a decade, who do not feel a sense of community, who are not owners but are employed and have enough money. This group typically feels less than safe in their central city, notice rubbish less and feel the council does not act in the city's best interests.

Table 4: Correlation matrix of urban pride arguments. New Zealand, 2008

		1	2	3	4	5	6	7	8	9	10
1	Female	1.00									
2	Health	0.04	1.00								
3	Duration	0.04	-0.01	1.00							
4	Community	*0.04*	0.04	0.03	1.00						
5	Owner	0.04	0.01	*0.06*	*0.09*	1.00					
6	Not employed	*0.12*	*-0.10*	0.05	*0.08*	-0.02	1.00				
7	Enough	0.01	*0.10*	0.04	0.01	*0.10*	-0.07	1.00			
8	Minority	-0.04	*-0.11*	*-0.14*	*0.06*	*-0.18*	-0.06	*-0.10*	1.00		
9	Safe	*-0.06*	*0.12*	0.00	0.01	*-0.05*	0.02	0.04	*-0.08*	1.00	
10	Clean	-0.03	0.02	*-0.05*	*0.04*	0.02	0.00	0.02	0.01	*0.11*	1.00
11	Council	0.00	0.03	*-0.05*	*0.09*	*-0.13*	0.03	0.02	*0.10*	*0.07*	*0.09*

Source: Quality of Life Survey, 2008.
Number of observations: Min 5957 to Max 6093.

5.2 The correlation matrix

The pairwise correlation matrix of the 11 variables listed above is reproduced in Table 4. Although the variance inflation factor was low at 1.05 and tolerances were all over 0.9, almost half the pairwise correlations were statistically significant ($p \leq 0.05$ in bold italics)[30].

The connections implied by this correlation matrix are instructive. Reading the statistically significant correlations by column shows that women (column 1) were more likely to feel a sense of community in their neighbourhood, were less likely to be employed, and felt less safe within the city centre during the day. From column 2 we learn that good health was associated with being employed, having enough money, being defined as European, and feeling safe. Column 3, duration, identifies those who lived in the city for a decade. They are more likely to be home owners, less likely to be employed or identify as a minority. They are also more likely to be critical of the city in terms of its cleanliness and the extent to which the council represents the interests of the majority.

Feeling a sense of community (column 4) is positively correlated with home ownership, not being employed, being a minority, seeing the city as clean, and feeling positive about council. Home ownership (column 5), is associated with having enough money and not being a minority, but also not feeling safe in the city centre or agreeing that council works in the best interests of the majority. Not being employed (column 6) is negatively associated with having enough money and not identifying with minority status. Having enough money (column 7) is a characteristic of minorities, as is feeling very safe in the city centre, but feeling less positive about council decisions. Identification with a minority is negatively correlated with feeling safe in the central city but positively associated with approval of council. Those who feel safe in the city also view the city as clean and have a positive view of council (column 9). Appreciating a clean city and viewing council positively are positively correlated (column 10).

The results of applying the random intercepts model (equation 3) are presented in Table 5. The results only include city random effects because the inter-ward intra-class correlation dropped to almost zero. In other words, ward to ward differences in urban pride were due almost entirely to population composition effects rather than to unique contexts characteristic of the wards themselves[31]. Cities, rather than wards within them, are the primary object of city pride as the city pride question itself implies.

The first point to note from the fixed effects estimates in Table 5 is that urban pride is most strongly associated with civic stake holding, and with the confidence people have that their council works in their best interests. Those supporting Council have a mean

---

[30]The Šidák correction used here takes multiple comparisons into account.

[31]In many applications of the multilevel model adding successive attributes of individuals absorbs some of the variance that occurs between level 2 groups. The variability in the ICC that takes place when variables are added can reflect an incomplete specification of the level 1 effects model.

Table 5: The distribution of urban pride. Stake holding fixed effects and city random effects. New Zealand, 2008

Variable	Description	Coef.	Std Err.	z	P > |z|
	FIXED EFFECTS				
Controls					
Female	Female	0.10	0.02	4.91	0.00
Health	Health good or very good	0.06	0.21	3.01	0.00
Emotional stakes					
Duration	Resident in city for 10 years or more	0.11	0.02	4.78	0.00
Community	Sense of community	0.24	0.02	11.22	0.00
Financial stakes					
Owner	Home owner	0.08	0.08	3.80	0.00
Not employed	Not employed	0.06	0.02	2.45	0.01
Enough	Income meets everyday needs	0.10	0.03	3.17	0.00
Cultural stakes					
Minority	Non-European	0.20	0.03	7.44	0.00
Civic stakes					
Safe	Feel safe in the central city	0.21	0.02	9.37	0.00
Clean	No rubbish noticed	0.23	0.02	11.20	0.00
Council	Confidence in council decisions	0.37	0.02	17.68	0.00
Constant		2.80	0.07	37.36	0.00
	RANDOM EFFECTS				
Cities	Constant	0.04	0.02		
	Residual	0.61	0.01		
Number of cases		5867			
Log likelihood		-6897.12			
LR vs linear model test		348.72			
Wald chi, pr=0		982.88			
Degrees of freedom		14			
AIC		13822.23			
Intraclass correlation		0.07			

Source: Quality of Life Survey, 2008.
Note: Estimates from the MIXED model, Stata14.

level of urban pride which is over one third (0.37%) of a unit higher than the rest of the population on the 1-5 urban pride scale. Those who feel a sense of community, see a clean city, and feel safe in its centre have a mean pride between a fifth and a quarter of a unit higher than the base population. Being non-European has a similar effect (0.20).

Having lived in the city for a decade or more has a weaker but still positive effect on urban pride, as does being female and being in good health. Having enough money to meet every day needs and being a homeowner are less important but still positive, increasing urban pride by at 0.10 and 0.08 of a unit, respectively. Being in retirement (most of those not employed) also contributes (0.06).

The model with covariates is a clear improvement over the null model with cities alone. In the absence of a clear equivalent of the r-squared statistic, R^2, I use the Akaike Information Criterion (AIC) $(-2 \log (\text{likelihood}) + 2k)$, where k is the number of model parameters and $-2 \log (\text{likelihood})$ is the deviance statistic. The difference between the null model and the model reported in Table 5 in AIC terms is 1901 = 15723-13822.

In summary, when it comes to accounting for the way urban pride varies over the population, the measures introduced to represent stake holding clearly matter. Urban

Table 6: Selected characteristics of the twelve New Zealand cities.

City	Pride	Population('000)	Affluence	European	Council
Rodney District	3.56	89.56	0.10	0.95	0.30
North Shore City	3.90	205.61	0.13	0.77	0.44
Waitakere City	3.62	186.44	0.07	0.67	0.48
Auckland City	3.48	404.66	0.14	0.62	0.40
Manukau City	3.33	323.97	0.07	0.46	0.51
Hamilton City	3.83	129.25	0.07	0.76	0.57
Tauranga City	3.87	103.64	0.06	0.88	0.40
Porirua City	3.57	48.55	0.10	0.66	0.51
Lower Hutt City	3.61	86.93	0.09	0.75	0.47
Wellington City	4.12	179.47	0.17	0.81	0.50
Christchurch City	3.82	348.44	0.07	0.88	0.41
Dunedin City	3.88	118.68	0.05	0.92	0.46

Source: Census of Population and Dwellings, 2006 and Quality of Life Survey, 2008.

pride is most sensitive to the degree to which council is recognised as listening to the people, a result which highlights the role of city leadership (Boezeman, Ellemers 2014). Feeling a sense of community, appreciating a clean city, and feeling safe in the city centre all contribute to a sense of urban pride as does being a member of an ethnic minority. Having a financial stake in the city (having enough income and being a homeowner) also matters but not to the degree anticipated.

6   City context

The results I have summarised from Table 5 suggest that urban pride reflects a sense of collective achievement rather than personal success. We might ask in addition whether cities themselves raise or lower urban pride. In the absence of an empirical literature on urban pride, I start with four relatively generic attributes of the city: its population size, its level of affluence, the share of Europeans in the population, and the confidence people have in its civic leadership. It is possible to think of a range of other measures such as the quality of the environment, but these will remain as suggested refinements only.

The distributions of the city's four characteristics are shown in Table 6 along with the average level of pride in each city. The population figure is drawn from the nearest population census (2006) as are the proportion of individuals with pre-tax incomes of over $70,000 per annum, and the proportion of Europeans in the city. The fourth variable, civic engagement, is aggregated from the sample responses.

The fixed effects coefficients at the individual level remained remarkably stable when each of these city level measures is added to the model singly or together. The exception is the variable 'minority' whose influence on urban pride drops as a result of the high concentration of the minority population in the two cities of Manukau and Porirua.

While the difference between the cities themselves may not account for much of the variance in urban pride, the contexts they represent may still condition the marginal effect of individual attributes. This tempering turns out to be the principle role of the city when it comes to understanding urban pride.

7   The multilevel model

Urban pride is a two-way street because it reflects attributes of both the residents *and* the characteristics of the city. However, while New Zealand cities do differ in size and composition, their differences appear to have little influence in raising or lowering urban pride. Rather, the role of the characteristics of the city is to modify the way particular forms of stake holding raise or lower urban pride.

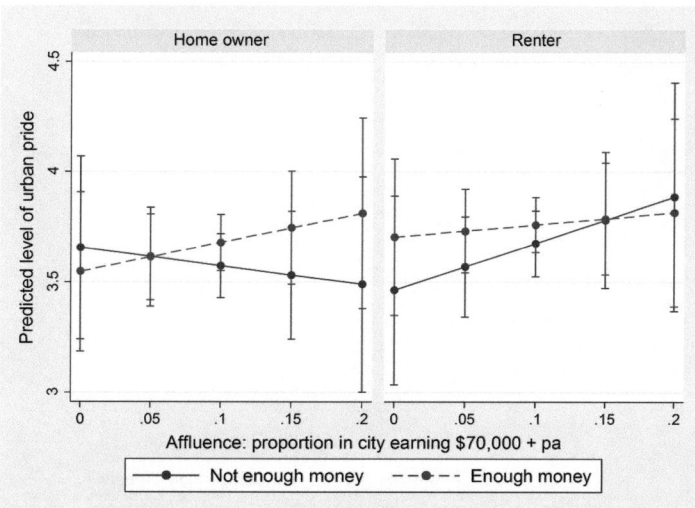

Source: Quality of Life Survey, 2008 and Census of Population and Dwellings, 2006.
Note: With the same fixed and random effects as in Table 5 adding the interaction of
enough x owner x affluence term yields a coefficient of -3.72 and a standard error of 1.91
and a z of -1.95 and $p > (z)$ of 0.052. The 95% confidence intervals are plotted.

Figure 4: The effect of 'not having enough money' on urban pride in more affluent cities
by housing tenure. New Zealand, 2008

I illustrate this last point by showing that the negative effect on urban pride of not
having enough money has greater effect in more affluent cities, that the level of urban
pride exhibited by minorities rises as their share of the population increases, and that
duration of residence modifies the way city-wide support of the local city council affects
urban pride. These do not exhaust the possible interactions between individuals and their
city of course, but they do indicate the way the city can influence the level of urban pride
people express.

7.1 The influence of context on financial stake holding

The motivation for the first of these illustrations is the possible role of relativities. The
argument here is that it is not just financial wellbeing that moderates one's pride in the
city but one's *relative* position. Recall from Table 6, that affluence at the city level is
measured as the proportion of the 2006 census population who earn more than $70,000
per annum (before tax). The range across New Zealand cities is quite wide, from a low of
five percent in Dunedin City through to 17 percent in the capital, Wellington City. The
testable proposition is that not having enough money 'to meet every day needs' may have
a greater negative effect on urban pride in more affluent cities because it is associated
with lower relative rank, over and above the pride reducing effects of material deprivation
itself. The secondary argument is that this relationship will vary with homeownership.

I have already shown that, as a characteristic of the city, affluence (a level 2 variable)
plays a very limited role in raising or lowering urban pride. However, when having enough
money (a level 1 variable) is interacted with city affluence separately for owners and
renters, renters without enough money (typically younger residents) return higher levels
of urban pride in cities which are more affluent. This result is apparent in the solid line
in the right panel of Figure 4. By contrast, homeowners without enough money (typically
older residents) return lower levels of urban pride in more affluent cities (solid line, left
panel of Figure 4).

By contrast, renters and owners who say they *have* enough money to meet daily
needs both return higher levels of urban pride in more affluent cities (the dashed lines
in Figure 4) with city affluence having a more marked influence on homeowners' urban
pride. The results presented in both panels of Figure 4 are plausible in light of the role I
have attributed to stake holding.

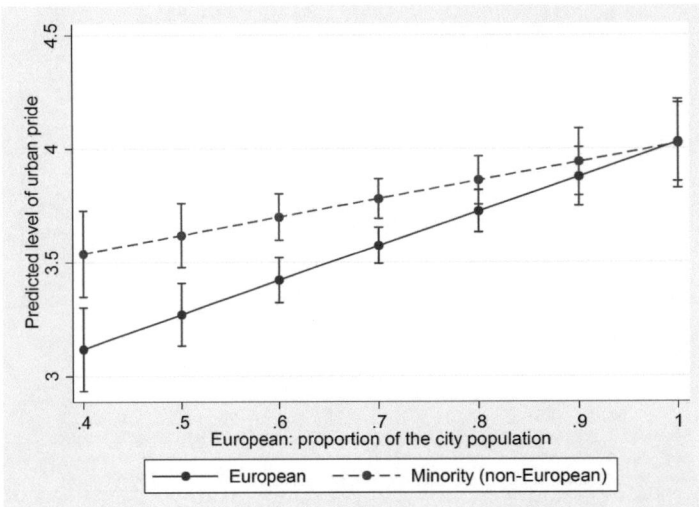

Source: Quality of Life Survey, 2008 and Census of Population and Dwellings, 2006.
Note: With the fixed effects of Table 5 in the model, the addition of the cross-level term
(minority x European) is $\beta = -0.710$ (SE=0.19; z= -3.74).

Figure 5: The positive impact of minority status on urban pride falls as the proportion of
Europeans in the city rises. New Zealand, 2008

7.2 Context influences on cultural stake holding

My second illustration addresses the impact minority ethnic status has on urban pride.
My expectation was that minorities would return higher levels of pride in cities the larger
their share of the population because the relative size of the minority groups have been
shown to contribute to both a greater sense of identity and collective strength (Tyler,
Blader 2001, p. 209–210). My expectation in the case of non-Europeans living in New
Zealand cities therefore was that their sense of identity would diminish as their share of
the population fell and this would be reflected in the level of pride they expressed in their
city. The evidence in this case rests on the interaction of the level 2 variable 'European'
and the level 1 variable 'minority'.

Figure 5 offers support for the minority 'share' hypothesis. The fixed effects results of
Table 5 have minorities returning higher levels of urban pride than the European majority.
Introducing a city x minority cross-level effect reveals how much urban pride rises as the
proportion of Europeans in the city increases. This rise is much slower in the case of
minorities (dashed line) and the urban pride converges when the proportion of Europeans
in the city approaches its maximum. In other words, while members of ethnic minorities
in New Zealand return higher levels of urban pride than the much larger number of
Europeans, any such difference falls as the proportion of Europeans rises, reflecting an
expected diminution in the social and cultural identity of non-Europeans.

7.3 Does the urban pride effect of support for Councils vary with duration of residence?

A third possible factor influencing urban pride is duration of residence. However, discerning
this interaction is more complicated because the relationship could conceivably be two-way.
The length of residence in a city could be a function of as well as an influence on pride:
being proud of the city may encourage staying, and those who are not particularly proud
of their city may be more likely to leave. The endogeneity present in this relationship
renders my investigation of this relationship quite exploratory.

Those who see City Councils acting in the interests of the majority return higher
levels of urban pride (as I showed in Table 5). However it is possible that this relationship
is affected by how long people have lived in the city. The available duration of residence
variable only separates those who are relatively new to the city, from those who have
lived there for more than a decade. (Finer partitions beyond the decade offered little

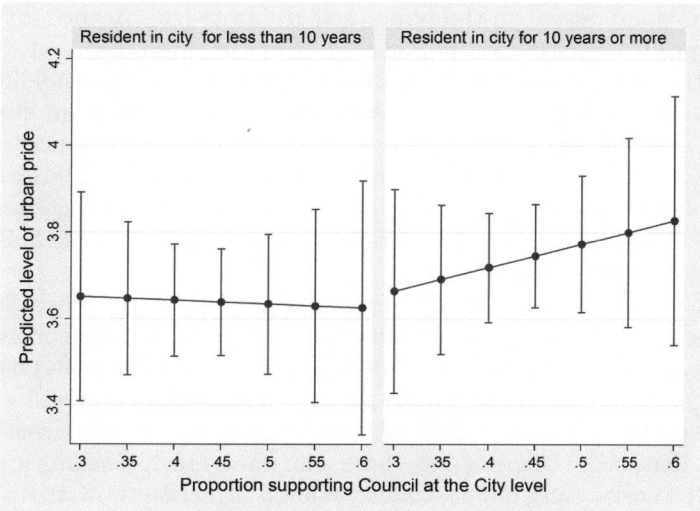

Source: Quality of Life Survey, 2008.
Note: The estimate of the Council x duration interaction term is $\beta = 0.631$ (se= 0.32), z = 1.97.

Figure 6: The estimated relationship between urban pride and city wide support for Council: longer vs. shorter term residents. New Zealand, 2008

further insight).

Figure 6, which interacts duration of residence with the proportion of the city supporting Council, suggests that the positive relationship between urban pride and the city's confidence in its council only applies to the longer term residents. The pride experienced by relative new comers in their city appears unaffected by the confidence the city has in its council. The 95% confidence intervals are relatively wide in this case but with the fixed effects of Table 5 in the model the interaction between the level 1 variable duration and the level 2 variable Council is statistically significant.

To summarise Section 7, when it comes to statistically accounting for the variance in the pride we express in our cities, city characteristics themselves account for relatively little. Most of the variance in urban pride comes down to the stake individuals have in their city. Having said that, exactly *how* people's stake in the city affects their level of urban pride is influenced by the characteristics of the city. Being able to demonstrate this contingency and the way in which city context modifies the effect of stake holding on urban pride is one of the primary findings of this paper, and the main reason for reporting the multilevel model.

8 Conclusions

Collins' recent study of pride in British cities suggested that, "civic pride has been under-theorised in geography and that the emotional meanings of pride need to be better understood" (Collins 2016, p. 185). I agree, and in response, I have drawn a distinction between *civic* pride as promulgated by city leaders and the emotion expressed by individual residents themselves which I have termed '*urban* pride'. Such a contrast is designed to expose the difference between city spokespersons claiming citizens are proud of their city and individuals who are free to express their own personal level of urban pride. The later has the value of demonstrating the way different levels of urban pride are distributed both within and between cities.

Civic pride in the sense above is a dimension of self-esteem which city politicians and planners go to great lengths to foster among their citizens. In practice however, most cities are content simply to anecdote civic pride when it suits, and few make a serious attempt to actually measure the level of urban pride empirically. New Zealand cities may have been an exception in this respect by ensuring that their Quality of Life Survey actually included a question on the pride their residents have in their city.

In this paper I have sketched in a theory of urban pride based on stake holding as it applies to the city. I identified four primary sources: the stake holding that accrues through emotional attachment to the city, financial investment in the city, cultural affiliation and civic engagement. I then specified a multilevel model in order to empirically test the relative influence of such stake holding on urban pride. By drawing on a large random sample from twelve cities in an otherwise relatively homogeneous country like New Zealand, I have been able to assess the degree to which the stake individuals have in the city influences how proud they feel.

As a result of the Urban Consortium funding a large sample of nearly 6000 residents in 2008, I have been able to show that certain types of stake holding have more influence than others. After controlling for gender and self-assessed health, individuals positively disposed towards their council, who felt safe and saw their city as clean and well maintained were more likely to declare such pride. This is also true of those who felt a sense of community. I also learned that, other things equal, those who owned their dwelling and who felt they earned enough to meet every day needs also enjoyed higher levels of urban pride. When it came to emotional stake holding, I was able to show that ethnic minorities return higher levels of urban pride as their share of the city population increased.

I went into this project expecting that the identified characteristics of cities themselves would have a major influence on the level of urban pride citizens report. This was not the case. Most of the measurable variance turned out to be due to individual stake holding. By explicitly testing for city x individual interaction (cross level effects) estimates from the multilevel model revealed that city characteristics *conditioned* the way individual stakes in the city influenced urban pride. They revealed how the negative effect on urban pride of not having enough money is more marked in more affluent cities, how the higher levels of urban pride exhibited by minorities increased as their share of the population in the city rose, and how duration of residence affects the way aggregate support of city councils conditioned citizens level of urban pride.

Although broader than Kenneth Boulding's proposition on stake holding, the above findings are consistent with his argument on pride and shame (Boulding 1987). At the same time my analysis has rested on a single definition of urban pride – pride in the 'look and feel of your city'. There are many other ways of asking about urban pride and if and when they are applied we may discover other ways in which stake holding alters the pride we hold in our cities.

Measures of urban pride have been argued to be among the 'soft' returns that accrue to accumulated investment in the city. If city leaders are tempted to use such 'soft' measures alongside the standard financial measures, then we need to know a great deal more about what people mean by urban pride, what generates the emotion, how it takes root and among whom, in what circumstances, and in what kinds of cities. As we have learned from the burgeoning literature on subjective wellbeing, investments in the community are unlikely to carry the force of change unless their returns can be measured (Stiglitz et al. 2009). So far, urban pride has remained a largely unmeasured response to our feelings toward our city and as such remains an unexploited barometer of the distributional consequences of public and private investment.

References

Anttiroiko AV (2015) City branding as a response to global intercity competition. *Growth and change* 46: 233–252. CrossRef.

Bell DA, de Shalit A (2011) *The spirit of cities. Why identity of a city matters in a global age.* Princeton University Press, Oxford

Bennett K (2013) Emotion and place promotion: passionate about a former coalfield. *Emotion, space and society* 8: 1–10. CrossRef.

Boezeman EJ, Ellemers N (2014) Volunteer leadership: the role of pride and respect in organisational identification and leadership satisfaction. *Leadership* 10: 160–173. CrossRef.

Boulding KE (1987) The economics of pride and shame. *Atlantic Economic Journal* 15: 10–19. CrossRef.

Collins T (2016) Urban civic pride and the new localism. *Transactions of the Institute of British Geographers* 41: 175–186. CrossRef.

Cummins RA (2009) The Australian Unity Wellbeing Index 2001-2008: variations in subjective wellbeing linked with major events and inflation. *Social Indicators Network News* 96: 1–4

Davidson J, Smith M, Bondi L (2007) *Emotional geographies.* Ashgate, Hamshire, UK. CrossRef.

Evans MDR, Kelley J (2002) National pride in the developed world: survey data from 24 nations. *International journal of public opinion research* 14: 304–336. CrossRef.

Fabrykant M, Magun V (2015) Grounded and normative dimensions of national pride in comparative perspective. Higher School of Economics Research Paper, National Research University Higher School of Economics, Moscow

Ferrer-i Carbonell A, Frijters P (2004) How important is methodology for the estimates of the determinants of happiness? *The Economic Journal* 114: 641–659. CrossRef.

Ha SE, Jang SJ (2015) National identity, national pride, and happiness: The case of South Korea. *Social Indicators research* 121: 471–482. CrossRef.

Haidt J (2003) The moral emotions. In: Davidson RJ, Scherer KR, Goldsmith HH (eds), *Handbook of affective sciences.* Oxford University Press, Oxford, England, 852–870

Helliwell JF, Putnam RD (2004) The social context of well-being. *Philosophical Transactions of the Royal Society B: Biological Sciences* 359: 1435–46. CrossRef.

Hosmer DW, Lemeshow S (2000) *Applied logistic regression.* John Wiley, Sons Ltd, New York. CrossRef.

Hox J (2002) *Multilevel analysis.* Lawrence Erlbaum Associates, Mahwah, NJ. CrossRef.

Jones K (1991) Specifying and estimating multi-level models for geographical research. *Transactions of the Institute of British Geographers* 16: 148–159. CrossRef.

Jones K, Johnston J, Pattie CJ (1992) People, places and regions: exploring the uses of multi-level modelling in the analysis of electoral data. *British Journal of Political Science* 22: 343–380. CrossRef.

Kelly J (1998) Attachment to one's city. *Australian Social Monitor* 1: 14–15

Kreft I, du Leeuw J (2006) *Introducing multilevel modelling.* London. CrossRef.

Kristoffersen I (2010) The metrics of subjective wellbeing: cardinal neutrality and additivity. *The Economic Record* 86: 98–123. CrossRef.

Lea SEG, Webley P (1997) Pride in economic psychology. *Journal of Economic Psychology* 18: 323–340. CrossRef.

Luke DA (2004) *Multilevel modelling*. Sage Publications, London. CrossRef.

McKelvey RD, Zovoina W (1975) A statistical model for the analysis of ordinal level dependent variables. *Journal of Mathematical Sociology* 4: 103–120. CrossRef.

Morrison PS (2007) Subjective well-being and the city. *Social Policy Journal of New Zealand* 30: 74–103

Morrison PS (2011) Local expressions of subjective well-being: the New Zealand experience. *Regional Studies* 45: 1039–1058. CrossRef.

Pachenkov O (2014) Review of: Da bell, a de-shalit (2011) why identity of a city matters in a global age. oxford: Princeton university press. *International Journal of Urban and Regional Research* 38: 366–368. CrossRef.

Pawlowski T, Downward P, Rasciute S (2014) Does national pride from international sporting success contribute to well-being? an international investigation. *Sport Management Review* 17: 121–132. CrossRef.

Quality of Life Team (2009) Quality of life survey 2008. National report, Nielsen, Wellington

Rabe-Hesketh S, Skrondal A (2008) *Multilevel and longitudinal modeling using Stata*. Stata Press, College Station, Texas. CrossRef.

Randall S (1995) City pride - from 'municipal socialism' to 'municipal capitalism'? *Critical Social Policy* 15: 40–59. CrossRef.

Reeskens T, Wright M (2011) Subjective well-being and national satisfaction: taking seriously the "proud of what?" question. *Psychological Science* 22: 1460–1462. CrossRef.

Reissland N (1994) The socialisation of pride in young children. *International journal of behavioural development* 17: 541–552. CrossRef.

Rosenblatt AD (1988) Envy, identification, and pride. *Psychoanalytic Quarterly* LVII: 56–71

Roskruge M, Grimes A, McCann P, Poot J (2013) Homeownership, social capital and satisfaction with local government. *Urban Studies* 18: 2517–2534. CrossRef.

Sengupta NK, Luyten N, Greaves LM, Osborne D, Robertson A, Armstrong G, Sibley C (2013) Sense of community in New Zealand neighbourhoods: a multi-level model predicting social capital. *New Zealand Journal of Psychology* 42: 36–45

Sevin HE (2014) Understanding cities through city brands: city branding as a social and semantic network. *Cities* 38: 47–56. CrossRef.

Smith TW, Kim S (2006) National pride in comparative perspective: 1995/96 and 2003/04. *International journal of public opinion research* 18: 127–136. CrossRef.

Stiglitz J, Sen A, Fitoussi J (2009) Report of the commission on the measurement of economic performance and social progress. Commission on the measurement of economic performance and social progress, Paris

Subramanian SV, Jones K, Duncan C (2003) Multilevel methods for public health research. In: Kawachi I, Berkan LF (eds), *Neighbourhoods and health*. Oxford University Press, Oxford, 65–111. CrossRef.

Sullivan G (2014a) Collective emotions, german national pride and the 2006 world cup. In: Sullivan G (ed), *Understanding collective pride and group identity: new directions in emotion theory, research and practice*. Routledge, New York

Sullivan GB (2014b) *Understanding collective pride and group identity: new directions in emotion theory, research and practice.* Routledge, New York

Sussmuth B, Heyne M, Maennig W (2010) Induced civic pride and integration. *Oxford Bulletin of Economics and Statistics* 72: 202–220. CrossRef.

Tajfel H, Turner JC (1979) An integrative theory of intergroup conflict. the social psychology of intergroup relations. In: S.Worchel WGA (ed), *The social psychology of intergroup relations.* Brooks/Cole, Monterery, CA, 33–47

Tracy JL, Robins RW (2004) Show your pride: evidence for discrete emotion expression. *Psychological Science* 15: 194–200. CrossRef.

Tracy JL, Robins RW (2007) Emerging insights into the nature and function of pride. *Current directions in psychological science* 16: 147–150. CrossRef.

Trueman M, Klemm M, Giroud A (2004) Can a city communicate? Bradford as a corporate brand. *Corporate communications: an international journal* 9: 317–330. CrossRef.

Tyler TR, Blader SL (2001) Identity and cooperative behaviour in groups. *Group processes and intergroup relations* 4: 207–226. CrossRef.

von Scheve C, Ismer S (2013) Towards a theory of collective emotions. *Emotion Review* 5: 406–413. CrossRef.

Waitt G (2001) The olympic spirit and civic boosterism: the Sydney 2000 Olympics. *Tourism Geographies* 3: 249–278. CrossRef.

Wellington Regional Council (2011) Wellington Region Genuine Progress Index (GPI: 2001-2010). Technical report, Wellington Regional Council, Wellington

Wilcox K, Kramer T, Sen S (2011) Indulgence or self control: a dual process model of the effect of incidental pride on indulgent choice. *Journal of Consumer Research* 38: 151–163. CrossRef.

Williams G (1995) Prospecting for gold; Manchester's city pride experience. *Planning Practice and Research* 10: 345–358. CrossRef.

Wood EH (2006) Measuring the social impacts of local authority events: a pilot study of a civic pride scale. *Internatiional Journal Nonprofit Voluntary Sector* 11: 165–179. CrossRef.

Zenker S, Rutter N (2014) Is satisfaction the key? the role of citizen satisfaction, place attachment and place brand attitude on positive citizenship behaviour. *Cities* 38: 11–17. CrossRef.

A   Appendix: Level 1 variables

The survey questions asked are as follows. The underlined responses are coded 1, the rest as zero.

Health Q29: In general how would you rate your health? Poor, fair, good, Very good, Excellent

Duration Q8: How many years have you lived in this city? Less than 1, 1-2, 2-5, 5-10, 10 years or more

Community-sense Q37: R2. I feel a sense of community with others in my local neighbourhood: Strongly agree, Disagree, Neither, Agree, Strongly Agree.

Owner Q57: Who owns the residence you live in? You own this house/flat/apartment, You jointly own this house/flat/apartment with other people, a family trust owns this house/flat/apartment, parents/other family members or partner own this house/flat/apartment, a private landlord who is not related to you owns this...., a local authority or city councils owns...., Housing New Zealand owns ..... Other State landlord owns...

Employment Q24: Which of the following best describes your current employment status? By employed I mean you undertake work for pay, profit or other income, or do any work in a family business without pay. Employed fulltime (for 30 or more hours per week), employed part time (for less than 30 hours per week), Not in paid employment and looking for work, not in paid employment and not looking for work (e.g. full-time parent, retired persons).

Enough Q35: Which of the following best describes how well your total income meets your everyday needs for things such as accommodation, food, clothing and other necessities? Have more than enough money, enough money, just enough money, not enough money.

Minority Q1: Can you please tell me which ethnic group or groups you belong to? European, Maori, Samoan (and other non-European).

SafeCC Q13: R4: Now thinking about issues of crime and safety, using a four point scale ranging from very unsafe, a bit unsafe, fairly safe to very safe, please tell me how safe or unsafe you would feel in the following situations. In your city centre during the day.

No rubbish Q17: R1.. Have any of the following been a problem in your city over the last twelve months? Rubbish or little lying on the streets: yes, no, don't know.

Conf_council Q21r3: Thinking about your local City or District Council. On a scale of one to five, where one is strongly disagree and [four is agree] and five is strongly agree, how would you rate the following: R3. Overall, I have confidence that the council makes decisions that are in the best interests of my city or district.

Source: Quality of Life Team, 2009

The Journal of ERSA
Powered by WU

Volume 3, Number 2, 2016, 47–60
DOI: 10.18335/region.v3i2.129

journal homepage: region.ersa.org

Cities and Inequality*

Alessandra Michelangeli[1], Eugenio Peluso[2]

[1] University of Milan-Bicocca, Milan, Italy (email: alessandra.michelangeli@unimib.it)
[2] University of Verona, Verona, Italy (email: eugenio.peluso@univr.it)

Received: 29 February 2016/Accepted: 22 August 2016

Abstract. We propose an innovative methodology to measure inequality between cities. If an even distribution of amenities across cities is assumed to increase the average well-being in a given country, inequality between cities can be evaluated through a multidimensional index of the Atkinson (1970) type. This index is shown to be decomposable into the sum of inequality indices computed on the marginal distributions of the amenities across cities, plus a residual term accounting for their correlation. We apply this methodology to assess inequality between Italian cities in terms of the distribution of public infrastructures, local services, economic and environmental conditions.

JEL classification: R11, R12, R23

Key words: Inequality, inequality aversion, social welfare, city

1 Introduction

Recent literature has shown that excessive inequality produces negative effects not only for disadvantaged individuals but also for a whole community. The State of the World's Cities Report by UN-Habitat (2008) established an international alert line corresponding to a Gini coefficient[1] value of 0.4. Several African and Latin American cities exhibit a value of Gini coefficient above this threshold[2]. High income inequality can have drastic consequences of economic, social, and political nature, such as lack of investment, protests and riots, and civil conflicts. In addition, high inequality may lead to the weak functioning of labor markets, inadequate investments in public services, or institutional and structural failures in income redistribution (UN-Habitat 2008)[3]. Given the importance of having an

---

*Financial support by the Italian Ministry of University and Research is gratefully acknowledged. The authors gratefully acknowledge the Osservatorio del Mercato Immobiliare for housing market data; the Fondazione Rodolfo De Benedetti for labour market data; and Istituto Tagliacarne for data about local amenities. An earlier version of the paper was presented at the 55th ERSA Congress in Lisbon. We would like to thank the participants at this conference for their useful comments. We thank the editor Paolo Veneri and two anonymous reviewers for their constructive comments. The usual disclaimer applies.

[1]The Gini coefficient is a measure of inequality varying from 0 (every individual received an equal share of income, then there is perfect equality) to 1 (one individual receives all the income, then there is perfect inequality).

[2]See UN-Habitat (2010) and Brambilla et al. (2015) for a world's selected city-ranking by Gini index for the year 2010.

[3]Brambilla et al. (2015) provide a deeper discussion on why excessive inequality can be harmful for a community.

even distribution of resources, or at most moderate levels of inequality, to the normal functioning of a community, in this paper we focus on inequality across cities because we are witnessing a dramatic increase of people living in urban areas over the last 60 years. According to United Nations and World Health Organization projections, while less than one-third of the world's population lived in cities in 1950, about two thirds of humanity is expected to live in urban areas by 2030 (UN-Habitat 2008, WHO-UN Habitat 2016). Local facilities and public goods available at the city-level may have an impact on individual well-being. As a result, there has been a growing interest on complementing income measures with the value of public goods and services that are available at the municipality, provincial, or regional level (Aaberge et al. 2010). Following a multidimensional approach, we consider inequality in terms of urban disparities, i.e. provincial capitals rather than in terms of differences across individuals. We propose an innovative methodology, which relies on the assumption that an even distribution of local goods and services across cities increases the average level of well-being in a given country. Due to the spatial nature of such goods and services, not all individuals in a society are equally exposed to the same quantities and qualities of them. Location choices are also driven by preferences for local public goods so even though these goods are not marketable, their impact on individual utility is capitalized in housing and labor markets. The hedonic approach is used to obtain a monetary evaluation of local public goods, named amenities, and defined as location specific characteristics with positive or negative effects on household's utility (Bartik, Smith 1987). People living in different cities face different amenities, and this generates inequalities across individuals in the level of welfare they locally perceive. The link between welfare and inequality in a multidimensional setting is captured by the Abul Naga, Geoffard (2006) index. We extend their methodology by endogenously determining the parameters of the index through a hedonic model referred to the housing and labor markets.

We employ our methodology to assess inequality between 103 Italian provincial (NUTS-3) capitals on the basis of a set of localized goods, such as public infrastructure, local services, economic, and environmental conditions. The proposed methodology allows to disentangle not only the effect of the distribution of each amenity on overall inequality, but also the effect of the joint distribution of amenities in determining overall inequality across cities.

The multidimensional inequality index turns out to display a value indicating that there are significant disparities between cities, mainly due to differences in the availability of services and infrastructure, in particular health services, economic conditions, transport infrastructure, and educational services. Environmental conditions and cultural amenities play a minor role in determining the overall level of inequality.

The paper is organized as follows. In Section 2 we present the theoretical framework by deriving the multidimensional inequality index from a social evaluation function having specific properties. Section 3 describes the data. Section 4 presents the results. Section 5 concludes the paper.

2 Framework

This section first shows how to obtain the multidimensional inequality index (Section 2.1). Then the Rosen (1979) and Roback (1982) model is briefly reviewed to show how implicit prices of amenities are determined (Section 2.2). Implicit prices are needed to endogenously determine the value of the multidimensional inequality index parameters.

2.1 Assessing multidimensional inequality

To derive the multidimensional inequality index, we proceed in two steps. First, we introduce a function measuring the level of well-being in a given city, provided by a bundle of k amenities[4]. Second, we aggregate the levels of well-being specific to each city in the simplest way, i.e. by considering their mean.

---

[4] Albeit well-being usually refers to individuals, we use this term instead of "livability" since the latter is unusual in economic literature. We also avoid using "quality of life", which usually refers to city rankings based on the monetary value of a selected bundle of amenities.

Let us consider n cities, indexed by $i = 1, \ldots, n$. Each city is endowed with k amenities, which are all strictly positive. The quantities owned by city i are denoted by the vector $\boldsymbol{z}_i = (z_{i1}, \ldots, z_{ij}, \ldots, z_{ik}) \in R^k_{++}$.

We assume that an increasing and concave function $w(\boldsymbol{z}_i)$ measures the social evaluation of well-being in city i, as a function of the available amenities, and we define the average evaluation function among the n cities as $W(\boldsymbol{z}_1, \ldots \boldsymbol{z}_n) = \frac{1}{n} \sum_{i=1}^{n} w(\boldsymbol{z}_i)$. The monotonicity of $w(\cdot)$ implies that an increase in the quantity of any amenity in any city results to be socially desirable. The concavity of $w(\cdot)$ implies inequality aversion, that is, it would be socially desirable having a homogeneous level of amenities across cities, rather than cities exhibiting huge disparities in terms of public goods, services, and infrastructure. Under the assumption of inequality aversion, society is willing to renounce a share of amenities to obtain an equitable distribution of them across cities. The higher inequality aversion, the higher the share society is willing to renounce. This idea was initially introduced in the risk literature by Pratt (1964) through the concept of "certainty equivalent", which is the amount of money a decision maker is willing to pay to undertake a risky decision. It is a function of the risk attitude of the decision maker. Atkinson (1970) imported in inequality and welfare measurement the notion of certainty equivalent by defining the analogous concept of "equally distributed equivalent income", which is the amount of income that, if equally distributed across individuals, would enable the society to reach the same level of welfare as the actual (unequal) distribution of incomes. The equally distributed equivalent income has been extended to the multidimensional case by Tsui (1995, 1999) (see also Gajdos, Weymark 2005, Abul Naga, Geoffard 2006; Weymark 2006 for a survey). In this paper, we transpose these concepts in comparing well-being among cities. More precisely, we define the vector of equally distributed equivalent amenities as the quantity of amenities that, if equally distributed across the n cities, guarantee the same average well-being as the (unequal) current amenity distribution.

Figure 1 shows the simple case with two cities: a and b, and two amenities: z_1 and z_2. We assume cities a and b are endowed with the bundles $Z_a = (Z_{1a}, Z_{2a})$ and $Z_b = (Z_{1b}, Z_{2b})$, respectively. The distribution of two amenities is unequal since city a has a greater quantity of amenity 2 and a lower quantity of amenity 1, compared with city b.

Let us define $Z_m = (Z_{1m}, Z_{2m})$ the mean bundle, containing the average quantity of each amenity, that is $Z_{1m} = (Z_{1a} + Z_{1b})/2$ and $Z_{2m} = (Z_{2a} + Z_{2b})/2$.

Jensen's inequality[5] implies that the level of social well-being would be higher if a and b were endowed with the same bundle of amenities Z_m rather than with their actual bundles Z_a and Z_b. In formal terms,

$$2W(Z_m) > W(Z_a) + W(Z_b). \tag{1}$$

By continuity and monotonicity of $W(\cdot)$, starting from (1) it is possible to find a positive scaling factor $\theta < 1$, such that the bundle $\theta Z_m = (\theta Z_{1m}, \theta Z_{2m})$ satisfies $2W(\theta Z_m) = W(Z_a) + W(Z_b)$. The vector θZ_m contains the equally distributed equivalent amenities mentioned above, which guarantee the same average level of well-being provided by the actual (unequal) amenity distribution across cities.

Abul Naga, Geoffard (2006) provide an axiomatic characterization of θ as an index of relative equality and its complement to one $(1 - \theta)$ as a (relative) index of inequality. While a formal presentation of their framework goes beyond the scope of this paper, we point out the assumptions needed to formulate the multidimensional inequality index $(1 - \theta)$, such that it can be used to measure inequality between cities. The social evaluation function is assumed to take a Cobb-Douglas form, $w(\boldsymbol{z}_i) = \prod_{j=1}^{k} z_{ij}^{\sigma_j}$. The parameter σ_j captures the aversion to an unequal distribution of amenity - across cities. In Section 2.1 we further discuss the role of this parameter in the setup and present the methodological strategy to determine the value of σ associated with each amenity.

---

[5]Jensen's inequality (Jensen 1906) states that for any strictly concave function u defined on a random variable X with expected value $E(x)$, we get $u(E(x)) > E(u(x))$. In social welfare theory, this means that, for any concave individual utility, the average welfare of an egalitarian distribution is always higher than the average welfare obtained through any other distribution of the same total amount of resources. In the example above Jensen's inequality refers to the distribution of urban amenities across cities a and b.

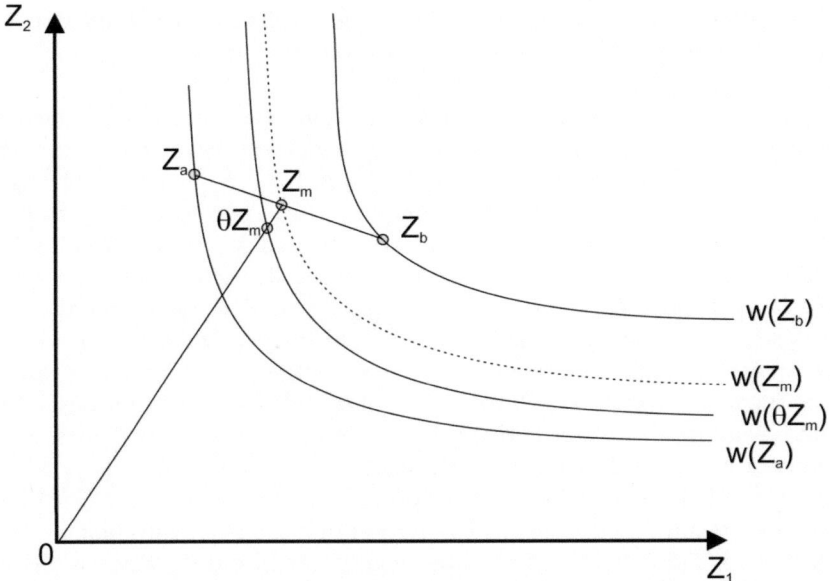

Figure 1: The equally distributed equivalent amount of amenities

The equality index θ has been shown to be decomposable into k indexes, one for amenity, related to the marginal distribution of amenities, and a residual term based on the dependence structure between amenities. In formal terms,

$$\left(\sum_{j=1}^{k} \sigma_j\right) \ln \theta = \sum_{k=1}^{k} \sigma_j \ln \gamma_j + \ln \rho \tag{2}$$

where γ_j, with $j 01, \ldots, k$ are k unidimensional indices of the Atkinson (1970) type, i.e. $\gamma_j = \frac{1}{\bar{z}_j} \left[\frac{1}{n} \sum_{i=1}^{n} z_{ij}^{\sigma_j} \right]^{\frac{1}{\sigma_j}}$; ρ is an interaction term equal to[6] $\rho = \frac{n^{k-1} \sum_{i=1}^{n} (\prod_{j=1}^{k} z_{ij}^{\sigma_j})}{\prod_{j=1}^{k} (\sum_{i=1}^{n} z_{ij}^{\sigma_j})}$.

The complement to 1 of γ_j, i.e. $1 - \gamma_j$, is the Atkinson index of inequality for amenity j. Notice that the value of parameters σ_j determines not only the degree of inequality aversion in the evaluation function $w(\cdot)$, but also the weight assigned to amenity j in the θ decomposition (1). In multidimensional inequality literature, equal weights are usually assumed for the different attributes under exam, as in the Human Development Index, as well as in studies by other institutions and scholars such as Becker et al. (2005) and Croci Angelini, Michelangeli (2012). In this paper, we follow Brambilla et al. (2013) to endogenously determine the values of σ_j. They are set to their respective weight on the monetary assessment of the amenity bundle with sample average quantities. The monetary value of amenities, denoted by p_j, with $j = 1, \ldots, k$, is determined on the basis of hedonic regressions based on the housing prices individuals are willing to pay and the wages they are willing to accept to locate in a given city. More precisely, σ_j, with $j = 1, \ldots, k$, is defined as:

$$\sigma_j = \frac{1 - \varepsilon_j}{k - 1} \tag{3}$$

where

$$\varepsilon_j = \frac{p_j \bar{z}_j}{\sum_{l=1}^{k} p_l \bar{z}_l} \tag{4}$$

Each parameter ε_j is set to be equal to the ratio between the estimated value of the average quantity of the amenity j and the value of all amenities. The methodology implicitly assumes that the higher the contribution of amenity j in determining the

---

[6]See Brambilla, Peluso (2010).

amenity bundle value, the more intense is the aversion for its uneven distribution across cities, the lower will be the value of σ_j.

In the next section, we determine the implicit prices of amenities, p_j, by referring to the hedonic spatial equilibrium model, developed by Rosen (1979) and Roback (1982), which explain the optimal location choice of agents, i.e. consumers and firms.

It is worth mentioning that implicit or shadow prices of amenities could be computed using alternative approaches. For example, Veneri, Murtin (2016), in order to compute multidimensional living standards among OECD regions, use the life satisfaction approach to estimate the shadow price of three dimensions of well-being: income, jobs, and health outcomes.

2.2 Determining the implicit value of amenities

Rosen (1979) considers household and business location decisions in order to maximize utility and to minimize costs, respectively. Household choices depend on the wage that one can earn living in a given city and the cost of living approximated by the cost of housing services. Households with a preference for amenity-rich cities will move to those cities, which are also the more expensive, and will be willing to earn lower wages to enjoy the higher (lower) level of amenities (disamenities). Conversely, household living in low-amenity cities will be compensated with higher wages and lower housing prices. In equilibrium, no-one has an incentive to move, since the relocation costs are higher than the utility gains generated by moving. The representative household experiences the same level of utility in all cities, and unit production costs are equal to the unit production price. Roback (1982) extends the model in a general equilibrium setting, by considering the housing market in addition to the labor market, since the two markets are interconnected and both contribute to determine the implicit price of amenities. The implicit price is given by the sum of the housing price differential and the negative of the wage price differential.

The model is empirically implemented by estimating two separate equations for the log of housing prices and wages:

$$\ln v_{hit} = \beta_0 + \beta_1 X_{hit} + \beta_2 Z_{it} + \eta_{hit} \tag{5}$$

$$\ln w_{mit} = \delta_0 + \delta_1 Y_{mit} + \delta_2 Z_{it} + \zeta_{mit} \tag{6}$$

where v_{hit} is the real price of housing unit h in city i at time t; X_{hit} is a vector of housing characteristics; Z_{it} is a vector of amenities in city i; w_{mit} is the real wage of individual m in city i at time t; Y_{mit} is a vector of individual characteristics; $\eta_{hit} \sim N(0; \sigma_\eta^2)$ and $\zeta_{mit} \sim N(0; \sigma_\zeta^2)$.

The implicit price of amenity z_j is given by

$$p_j = \frac{\partial v}{\partial z_j} - \frac{\partial w}{\partial z_j}. \tag{7}$$

3 Data

We use our methodology to assess inequality between 103 provincial capitals observed in the period 2001-2010. We consider six amenities: cultural infrastructure, educational and health services, transport infrastructure; economic and environmental conditions (Table A.1 in the Appendix sets out the list of amenities with their sources). Cultural conditions, educational services and health services are measured each by an index provided by GuglielmoTagliacarne Institute at the provincial level in 2004. These three indices are used as proxy for services at the city-level. Each of these indices is set to 100 for the Italian average. Cultural conditions are measured by an index of cultural infrastructure accounting for museums, theatres, cinemas, libraries, gyms. The index for educational services combines information about the number of schools of all levels, public and private; the number of classrooms per school; presence of building facilities, such as recreation and gym facilities, library and computer lab facilities; the number of teachers. The index

Table 1: Summary statistics of amenity variables

Variable	Mean	Std. Dev.	Min.	Max.	Unit of observation	Year
Cultural infrastructure	126.11	71.89	18.90	504.17	Province	2004
Educational services	113.47	41.34	24.06	325.32	Province	2004
Health services	121.75	56.90	26.59	287.19	Province	2004
Transport	105.29	26.88	47.00	161.00	Municipality	2006
Employment rate	90.33	7.39	68.61	97.23	Municipality	2010
Air quality	9.96	3.12	0.00	18.00	Municipality	2004

for health services aggregates statistical information about the number of doctors at all levels, the number of nurses and other auxiliary personnel, the number of hospital beds, and the number and types of medical devices. Transport infrastructure is measured by a multimodal index that considers accessibility by air, train and car. The index is at the city level and is set equal to 100 for the European average. It is provided for the year 2006 by European Observation Network for Territorial Development and Cohesion (ESPON) project. The employment rate serves as proxy for economic conditions. The rate is at the city level for the year 2010, and it is provided by the Italian National Institute of Statistics (ISTAT). Environmental conditions are represented by the air quality in terms of reduced number of polluting agents in the air. The variable for air quality was constructed setting the maximum number of air-polluting observed in our sample equal to zero and associating increasing integer values with the decreasing number of air-polluting agents. The numbers of polluting agents are at the city level, refer to 2004 and were from ISTAT. Table 1 presents summary statistics of amenity variables.

The 103 provincial capitals of our sample have on average a higher endowment of cultural infrastructure, followed by health and educational services. The indicator for cultural infrastructure shows the largest variability, according the standard deviation, followed by health and educational services.

For the housing and labor markets, we use the same data set of Colombo et al. (2014) used to measure quality of life in the 103 cities. Housing market data are from the Real Estate Observatory of the Italian Ministry of Finance, and refer to individual house transactions in the 103 Italian provincial capitals between 2004 and 2010. In addition to sale prices, the dataset provides a detailed description of housing characteristics, such as total floor area, number of bathrooms, floor level, number of garages, location (center, semi center, suburb), and location (center, semi-center, suburbs).

Labor market data are from the Italian National Social Security Institute (INPS) for years 2001 and 2002 and were provided by Fondazione Rodolfo De Benedetti. The dataset provides information on the private sector employees' annual earnings, the level of occupation, whether the job is full-time or part-time, contract length, province of work, and sector of economic activity. Personal and demographic characteristics include gender, age, nationality, and province of residence. Housing prices and wages are measured at constant 2004 prices. As mentioned in Colombo et al. (2014), the difference in the timing of the data between wages and housing prices is due to data availability. However considering that we are using only data on dependent employment (entrepreneurs and self-employed are not included) the cross-sectional variation across cities is relatively stable over time, and the actualization procedure applied to the data should account for the possible concerns on this issue[7].

---

[7]We computed the times-series and cross-sectional variation of housing prices and wages. It turns out that the latter is much larger than the former for both variables. For housing prices, the proportion of between variation is about 90 per cent and the proportion of within variation is about 10 per cent. For wages, the proportion of between variation is about 97 per cent and within variation is about 3 per cent.

Table 2: Amenity hedonic prices and multidimensional inequality index decomposed in the six unidimensional inequality indices plus an interaction term

Variable	Hedonic price* p_j	Parameter measuring inequality aversion** σ_j	Univariate inequality index $1 - \gamma_j$
Cultural infrastructure	7	0.1956	0.4104
Education	122	0.1310	0.2482
Health services	91	0.1448	0.3270
Transport	76	0.1601	0.2560
Employment rate	68	0.1694	0.2783
Air quality	21	0.1989	0.2309
Interaction term $\rho = \dfrac{n^{k-1}\sum_{i=1}^{n}(\prod_{j=1}^{k} z_{ij}^{\sigma_j})}{\prod_{j=1}^{k}(\sum_{i=1}^{n} z_{ij}^{\sigma_j})}$		1.3860	
Multidimensional Inequality Index $I = 1 - \theta$		0.3121	

*The implicit price is the marginal willingness to pay (in Euro at constant 2004 prices) associated with a one-standard deviation in the corresponding amenity.

**Higher values of σ_j imply lower levels of inequality aversion.

4 Results

Equations (5) and (6) are estimated by OLS and the results are reported in Table A.1 and A.2, respectively, in the Appendix. Robust standard errors are used with clustering at city level in order to allow for within-city correlation. The covariates used in model (5) account for about 72 per cent of the variance of the logarithm of housing prices, while the marginal explanatory power of local amenities is about 7%. Model (6) explains 61 per cent of the variability of the logarithm of wages, while the marginal explanatory power of local amenities is about 1.8%. The amenity coefficients are jointly statistically significant in the two models ($F = 15.01$, $p < 0.00$ for the housing price equation; $F = 37.46$, $p < 0.00$ for the wage equation).

Full implicit prices for local amenities are shown in Table 2, column 2. The implicit price of amenity z_j is given by (7). To calculate the first derivative, the estimated expected housing price and wage are obtained by (5) and (6), respectively. However, since the empirical specification for the housing price regression and wage regression are log-linear, the relation between the normal and the lognormal distribution has to be taken into account to derive appropriate estimates. The following results from the normal distribution are used. If Y is a normally distributed random variable with expected value μ and variance σ^2, $P = \exp(Y)$ is lognormally distributed with expected value equal to $\exp(\mu + \sigma^2/2)$. Hence, the expected values of housing price and wages have been obtained by plugging in the estimated values in the previous formulas.

The implicit price of a given amenity can be interpreted as the monetary amount, expressed in Euro at constant 2004 prices, households would be willing to pay annually for a one-standard deviation change in that amenity. Increasing the index for educational services by one-standard deviation is valued €122, while the implicit prices associated with health services and cultural infrastructure are €91 and €7, respectively. The weakness of the influence of culture on housing and labor markets is common in hedonic studies on Milan and other Italian cities (for instance Colombo et al. 2014, Brambilla et al. 2013). This is a puzzling result demanding a deeper investigation. The estimated marginal willingness to pay for increasing the employment rate by one-standard deviation is €68. Increasing the ESPON index for transport infrastructure by one-standard deviation is valued €76. A marginal improvement in air quality is valued €21.

The amenity estimated implicit prices and the city average quantities are used to

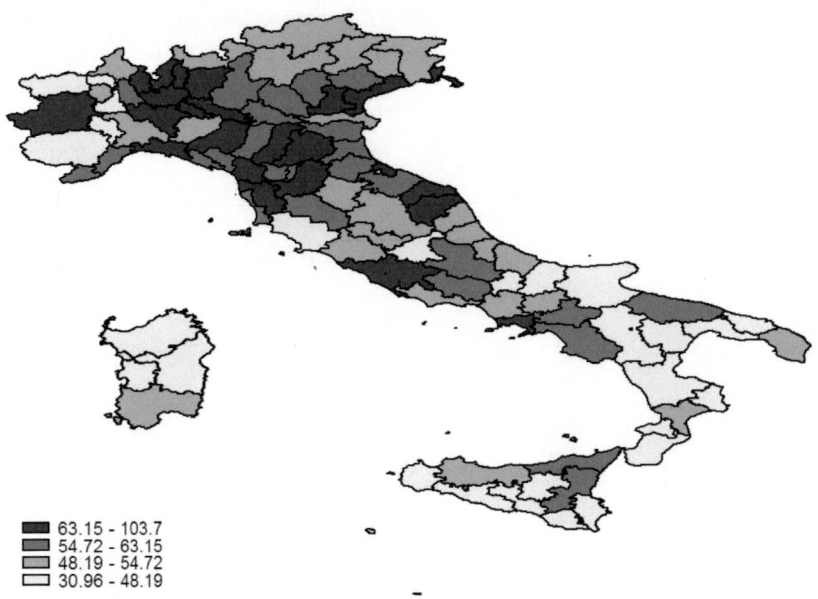

Figure 2: Distribution of W values across cities

estimate the vector of parameters $\boldsymbol{\sigma} = (\sigma_1, \ldots, \sigma_k)$ according to equations (5) and (6). We recall that their values, reported in Table 2, column 3, determine the level of inequality aversion and the weight of each amenity in the θ decomposition, given by equation (2). The higher σ_j, with $j = 1, \ldots, k$, the lower aversion to an unequal distribution of amenity j across cities, and the lower the value of the unidimensional inequality index for this amenity , i.e. $1 - \gamma_j$. The highest degree of inequality aversion is for educational and health services, followed by transport infrastructure and economic conditions, represented by the employment rate. Inequality aversion is lower for air quality and cultural amenities.

The last column of Table 2 shows the unidimensional inequality index of the Atkinson (1970) type, $1 - \gamma_j$. It is lower for air quality and becomes progressively higher for educational services, transport infrastructure, employment rate, health services and cultural infrastructure.

As mentioned in Section 2, ρ measures the effect on inequality due to the interdependence relationship between amenities. If ρ equals one, there is no joint effect of amenities on the multidimensional inequality index; if ρ is less than 1, the joint effects tend to magnify, while if ρ is more than 1, they offset each other. Table 2 shows a value for ρ higher than 1 implying that the joint effect of amenities contributes to the decrease of inequality across cities.

Finally, the multidimensional inequality index (3) turns out to be equal to 0.3121.

To sum up, overall inequality is mainly due to educational and health services, transport infrastructure, and economic conditions because of the higher inequality aversion and the higher value of the unidimensional inequality index for the variables associated with these four amenities. Air quality and cultural infrastructure play a minor role in determining the overall degree of inequality either because the unidimensional inequality index and the degree of inequality aversion are low, as for air quality, or because the inequality aversion and the weight of the variable are low, as for cultural amenities.

We use the estimated values for $\boldsymbol{\sigma} = (\sigma_1, \ldots, \sigma_k)$ to calculate the values of the evaluation function $W = \frac{1}{n} \prod_{j=1}^{k} z_{ij}^{\sigma_j}$ specified in Section 2, which gives the level of well-being individuals enjoy from the endowment of the six amenities specific to each city. Table 3 reports the city-ranking for the value function W, and Figure 2 shows the geographic distribution of W values across Italian cities. Looking at the map, a clear North-South divide can be observed. A clustering of high scores can be observed for cities in the Lombardy and Veneto regions. Cities in the South generally display relatively lower values of W, with clustering of low scores in the cities of Molise, Sardinia and Basilicata. Looking at the city size, well-being is generally higher in large cities (Rome,

Table 3: City ranking according to W values

City	W	City	W	City	W	City	W
Trieste	103.65	Forli	62.62	Biella	54.62	Asti	47.96
Firenze	97.28	Vicenza	62.58	Ascoli Piceno	54.57	Reggio Calabria	47.33
Roma	88.56	Brescia	61.95	Rovigo	54.08	Cosenza	46.81
Milano	85.48	Pistoia	61.59	Chieti	53.90	Vibo Valentia	45.56
Padova	81.92	Bari	61.17	Palermo	53.68	Sassari	45.51
Pisa	81.35	Novara	60.82	Viterbo	53.40	Ragusa	45.29
Napoli	80.36	Verona	60.43	Lecce	53.36	Cuneo	44.84
Varese	76.02	Livorno	60.20	Pescara	53.13	Trapani	44.41
Pavia	74.84	Prato	59.84	Cagliari	52.88	Campobasso	43.31
Bologna	73.20	Imperia	59.73	Caserta	52.49	Vercelli	43.01
Gorizia	72.88	La Spezia	59.62	Latina	52.09	Taranto	42.91
Lucca	70.29	Savona	59.41	Benevento	52.05	Isernia	42.23
Rimini	69.62	Massa	59.24	Udine	51.47	Oristano	41.93
Ancona	69.41	Catania	58.44	Pordenone	50.71	Aosta	41.80
Venezia	69.06	Ravenna	58.30	Alessandria	50.54	Siracusa	41.75
Torino	69.01	Mantova	58.25	Verbania	50.35	Potenza	41.17
Cremona	68.79	Ferrara	57.58	Trento	50.20	Rieti	40.41
Modena	68.22	Avellino	57.38	Bolzano	49.97	Foggia	39.05
Bergamo	67.01	Frosinone	57.29	Piacenza	49.73	Agrigento	37.24
Como	66.23	Treviso	56.68	Belluno	49.61	Crotone	36.50
Macerata	65.57	Siena	56.67	Teramo	49.35	Caltanissetta	36.19
Lecco	65.13	Salerno	56.45	Catanzaro	49.00	Grosseto	36.11
Genova	64.70	Messina	55.63	Sondrio	48.79	Enna	35.34
Lodi	63.88	L'Aquila	55.19	Arezzo	48.30	Matera	33.10
Parma	63.17	Reggio Emilia	54.80	Terni	48.23	Nuoro	30.95
Pesaro	63.14	Perugia	54.71	Brindisi	48.19		

Table 4: Ranking of Italian regions by W

Region	W	Region	W
Lazio	85.10	Umbria	52.70
Friuli Venezia Giulia	78.57	Abruzzo	52.44
Lombardy	76.87	Sicily	51.66
Campania	73.97	Apulia	50.71
Tuscany	70.47	Trentino Alto Adige	50.09
Veneto	66.97	Sardinia	47.03
Emilia Romagna	65.14	Calabria	45.99
Marche	64.17	Molise	42.99
Liguria	63.46	Aosta Valley	41.80
Piedmont	63.16	Basilicata	37.43

Milan, Naples) or medium-sized cities (Trieste, Firenze, Padua, Pisa).

The North-South divide is also evident if we aggregate the results for W by region, as shown in Table 4. The value of W corresponds to the average of provincial values by region, weighted by population size. The first ten regions with a higher value of W are located in the Center-North, with the exception of Lazio and Campania. The last ten are in Southern Italy, with the exception of Trentino Alto Adige and Aosta Valley.

Ferrara, Nisticò (2013) find similar results by measuring well-being at the regional level over about the same period of our analysis, from 1998 to 2008, using two composite indexes: the Augmented Human Development Index (AHDI), which is an adapted version of the Human Development Index for developed countries; the Well-Being Index (WBI), which extends the AHDI, by considering three important dimensions of well-being, i.e. equal opportunities as regards gender and age in the labor market, the ability to innovate and compete in the market, the quality of the socio-institutional context. The two rankings determined according to the values of AHDI and WBI show a sharp demarcation between the Center-North and Southern regions, which is less marked in the WBI ranking.

Finally, we compare the ranking of 103 Italian provinces based on well-being with the ranking of the same provinces based on per-capita GDP.[8] The Spearman's rank correlation coefficient, equal to 0.5888 ($P > |t| = 0.0000$), indicates a statistically significant positive relationship between these two measures. This means that our analysis is consistent with a unidimensional analysis based only on a measure of income. The advantage of a multidimensional approach is that it provides relevant insights about the factors underlying urban disparities.

5   Conclusion

A huge and multidisciplinary literature has analyzed the distribution of the main factors affecting people well-being across different communities (country, region, urban area). Traditional studies focus on income or wealth distribution. Some recent attempts consider other factors influencing well-being in addition to income. For example, Aaberge et al. (2013) take into account public service provision, such as health insurance or education. This paper is the first attempt to focus on inequality between cities, by setting a multidimensional framework. The multidimensional index we propose allows, on one hand, to separate the effect of different amenities, which contribute to determine the overall degree of inequality, and, on the other hand, to consider the joint effect of all amenities on the overall inequality. Moreover, our methodology allows the determination of some important aspects from a policy maker's point of view, such as the degree of inequality aversion specific to each amenity, and the weight of each amenity.

The methodology has been applied to measure inequality between the main Italian cities referring to six important factors. Our results show that to decrease inequality between cities, improving efficiency and equalizing opportunities and life-chances, policies favoring a more even availability of educational and health services, transport infrastructure and employment opportunities should be promoted. In this perspective, our methodology could be applied for simulating the effects of changes in the provision of local public goods on inequality. This constitutes a promising avenue for future research.

References

Aaberge A, Bhullera M, Langørgena A, Mogstad M (2010) The distributional impact of public services when needs differ. *Journal of Public Economics* 94: 549–562. CrossRef.

Aaberge R, Langorgen A, Lindgren P (2013) The distributional impact of public services in european countries. Eurostat methodologies and working papers, European Commission, Luxembourg

Abul Naga R, Geoffard PY (2006) Decomposition of bivariate inequality indices by attributes. *Economic Letters* 90: 362–367. CrossRef.

Atkinson A (1970) On the measurement of inequality. *Journal of Economic Theory* 3: 244–263. CrossRef.

Bartik TJ, Smith VK (1987) Urban amenities and public policy. In: Mills ES (ed), *Handbook of Regional and Urban Economics, vol. II.* Elsevier, Amsterdam, 1207–1254. CrossRef.

Becker GS, Philipson TJ, Soares RR (2005) The quantity and quality of life and the evolution of world inequality. *American Economic Review* 95: 277–291. CrossRef.

Brambilla MR, Michelangeli A, Peluso E (2013) Equity in the city: On measuring urban (ine)quality of life. *Urban Studies* 50: 3205–3224. CrossRef.

Brambilla MR, Michelangeli A, Peluso E (2015) Cities, equity and quality of life. In: Michelangeli A (ed), *Quality of Life in Cities: Equity, Sustainable Development and Happiness from a Policy Perspective.* Routledge Advances in Regional Economics, Science and Policy, 91–109

---

[8]Data on per capita GDP by province are from ISTAT and refer to year 2004.

Brambilla MR, Peluso E (2010) A remark on "Decomposition of bivariate inequality indices by attributes" by Abul Naga and Geoffard. *Economic Letters* 108: 100. CrossRef.

Colombo E, Michelangeli A, Stanca L (2014) La dolce vita: Hedonic estimates of quality of life in Italian cities. *Regional Studies* 48: 1404–1418. CrossRef.

Croci Angelini E, Michelangeli A (2012) Axiomatic measurement of multidimensional well-being inequality: Some distributional questions. *Journal of Behavioral and Experimental Economics* 41: 548–557

Ferrara AR, Nisticò R (2013) Well-being indicators and convergence across Italian regions. *Applied Research in Quality of Life* 8: 15–44. CrossRef.

Gajdos T, Weymark JA (2005) Multidimensional generalized Gini indices. *Economic Theory* 26: 471–496. CrossRef.

Jensen JLWV (1906) Sur les fonctions convexes et les inégalités entre les valeurs moyennes. *Acta Mathematica* 30: 175–193. CrossRef.

Pratt JW (1964) Risk aversion in the small and in the large. *Econometrica* 32: 122–136. CrossRef.

Roback J (1982) Wages, rents, and the quality of life. *Journal of Political Economy* 90: 1257–78. CrossRef.

Rosen S (1979) Wage-based indexes of urban quality of life. In: Mieszkowsi P, Stratzheim M (eds), *Current issues in urban economics*. John Hopkins Press, Baltimore, 74–104

Tsui KY (1995) Multidimensional generalizations of the relative and absolute inequality indices: The Atkinson-Kolm-Sen approach. *Journal of Economic Theory* 67: 251–265. CrossRef.

Tsui KY (1999) Multidimensional inequality and multidimensional generalized entropy measures: an axiomatic derivation. *Social Choice and Welfare* 16: 145–157. CrossRef.

UN-Habitat – United Nations Human Settlements Programme (2008) *State of the World's Cities 2008/2009, Harmonious Cities*. Earthscan, London

UN-Habitat – United Nations Human Settlements Programme (2010) *State of the World's Cities 20010/2011, Harmonious Cities*. Earthscan, London

Veneri P, Murtin F (2016) Where is inclusive growth happening? Mapping multidimensional living standards in OECD regions. OECD statistics working papers, 2016/01, OECD Publishing, Paris. CrossRef.

Weymark JA (2006) The normative approach to the measurement of multidimensional inequality. In: Farina F, Savaglio E (eds), *Inequality and Economic Integration*. Routledge, New York

WHO-UN Habitat – World Health Organization and United Nations Human Settlements Programme (2016) Global report on urban health. World Health Organization, Switzerland

A Appendix

Table A.1: Description and sources of amenity variables

Variable	Description	Source
Cultural infrastructure	Index of cultural infrastructure. Italian average = 100	Istituto Tagliacarne http://istitutotagliacarne.it
Educational services	Index of educational services. Italian average = 100	Istituto Tagliacarne http://istitutotagliacarne.it
Health services	Index of health services. Italian average = 100	Istituto Tagliacarne http://istitutotagliacarne.it
Transport	Multimodal accessibility index (train, air, car). European average = 100	ESPON http://espon.eu
Employment rate	Percentage rate	ISTAT
Air quality	Reduced number of polluting agents in the air	ISTAT

Table A.2: Estimation results for the housing price equation

Variable	Coefficient (Std. Err.)
Cultural infrastructure	0.00028 ***
	(0.00004)
Educational services	0.0035 **
	(0.0010)
Health services	0.0019 ***
	(0.00042)
Transport	0.0036 ***
	(0.00038)
Employment rate	0.0062 **
	(0.0027)
Air quality	0.00096 *
	(0.0004)
Total floor area (log)	0.8595 ***
	(0.02794)
Second bathroom	0.0596 ***
	(0.0069)
Third bathroom or more	0.0042 ***
	(0.00042)
To be renewed	-0.116 ***
	(0.0142)
Heating	0.0147 ***
	(0.0013)
2nd floor or higher	0.0183 ***
	(0.0012)
Parking	0.0723 ***
	(0.0080)
Elevator	0.0647 ***
	(0,0118)
Ln(age)	-0.0074 *
	(0.0039)
Location: central	0.1163 ***
	(0.0068)
Location: semi-central	0,0637 ***
	(0.0049)
Year 2005	0.0305 ***
	(0.0012)
Year 2006	0.0687 ***
	(0.0137)
Year 2007	0.0895 ***
	(0.01772)
Year 2008	0.0976 ***
	(0.0186)
Year 2009	0.1035 ***
	(0.01877)
Year 2010	0.1145 ***
	(0.0179)
R^2	0.8011
Adjusted R^2	0.8002
Number of observations	150,622

Significance levels are denoted with *** (1%), ** (5%), and * (10%)

Table A.3: Estimation results for the wage equation

Variable	Coefficient (Std.Err.)
Cultural infrastructure	-0.000043 *
	(0.00002)
Educational services	-0.0021 **
	(0.0010)
Health services	-0.00106 *
	(0.00068)
Transport	-0.00076 *
	(0.00039)
Employment rate	-0.0011 **
	(0.00056)
Air quality	-0.00091 *
	(0.0006)
Sex	0.1993 ***
	(0.0015)
Age	0.0307 ***
	(0.0005)
Age squared	-0.0002 ***
	(0.000006)
Country of birth: Asia	-0.1224 ***
	(0.0078)
Country of birth: Africa	-0.1292 ***
	(0.0048)
Country of birth: South America	-0.1053 ***
	(0.0034)
Executives	1.5548 ***
	(0.0076)
Managers and white collars	0.4641 ***
	(0.0038)
Agriculture	0.4958 ***
	(0.0107)
Electricity	0.3670 ***
	(0.0097)
Chemistry	0.3428 ***
	(0.0094)
Metalworking	0.2840 ***
	(0.0095) ***
Food, textile, wood	0.2289 ***
	(0.0096)
Building materials	0.2440 ***
	(0.0094)
Commerce and services	0.2919 ***
	(0.0098)
Transport and communications	0.3460 ***
	(0.0095)
Credit insurance	0.2636 ***
	(0.0096)
Firm size	0.0002 ***
	(0.0001)
Year 2002	0.0195 ***
	(0.0012)
Intercept	6.1977 ***
	(0.0635)
R^2	0.6140
Adjusted R^2	0.6089
Number of observations	165,917

Significance levels are denoted with *** (1%), ** (5%), and * (10%)